Diving and Snorkeling Guide to

The
Channel
Islands

by Dale and Kim Sheckler
and the editors of Pisces Books

 Pisces Books • New York

Acknowledgments

In the creation of this book the authors very much appreciate the assistance of the owners and crews of the dive boats *Truth, Conception, Vision, Peace, Scuba Luv'er, Spectre, Barbara Marie, Excalibur, Golden Doubloon, Cee Ray, Wild Wave, Mr. C, The Last Bite, Sand Dollar* and *Bottom Scratcher.* The authors would also like to thank Mary Lou Reed, David Reed, Leona Reed, Darren Douglass and the staffs of the dive stores of Southern California.

Publishers Note: At the time of publication of this book, all the information was determined to be as accurate as possible. However, when you use this guide, new construction may have changed land reference points, weather may have altered reef configurations, and some businesses may no longer be functioning. Your assistance in keeping future editions up-to-date will be greatly appreciated.
Also, please pay particular attention to the diver rating system in this book. Know your limits!

Library of Congress Cataloging in Publication Data
Sheckler, Dale.
  Diving and snorkeling guide to the Channel Islands.

  Includes index.
  1. Scuba diving -- Channel Islands -- Guide-books.
2. Skin diving -- Channel Islands -- Guide-books.
3. Channel Islands (Calif.) -- Description and
travel -- Guide-books. I. Sheckler, Kim.
II. Pisces Books (Firm)   III. Title.
GV840.S78S45   1986   917.94'9   86-30328

ISBN 0-86636-076-X

Photos: All photographs are by the author unless otherwise noted.

Color separations by
Hongkong Scanner Craft
Company Ltd., Hong Kong

Printed in Hong Kong

10 9 8 7 6 5 4 3 2 1

STAFF

Publisher	**Herb Taylor**
Project Director	**Cora Sibal Taylor**
Executive Editor	**Virginia Christensen**
Editor	**Joanne Bolnick**
Art Director	**Richard Liu**
Art/Prod. Coordinator	**Jeanette Forman**
Artist	**Daniel Kouw**

Table of Contents

How to Use This Guide

Diving California's Channel Islands is one of the most unique diving experiences in the world. Nothing can compare to diving in the crystal-blue wonderland of a kelp forest. This dive guide will acquaint you with the various dive sites around the California Channel Islands and will provide you with the general information you need to match a dive site to your particular diving skills. This guide will also give you a brief history and geography lesson on the Islands as well as show you how to hook-up with the services every diver needs such as charter boats and dive shops.

Rating System for Divers and Dives

Our suggestions as to the minimum level of expertise required for any given dive site should be taken in a conservative sense, keeping in mind the old adage about there being old divers and bold divers but no old bold divers. We consider a *novice* to be someone in decent physical condition, who has recently completed a basic certification diving course, or a certified diver who has not been diving recently or who has no experience in diving California waters. Several dive sites covered in this book are good for the novice diver but any time a beginning diver is new to California waters, we recommend that the diver be supervised by a knowledgeable divemaster or instructor as diving here is quite unique. Nearly all dive charter boats running to the islands have on board a suitable divemaster who can answer your questions. We consider an *intermediate* to be a certified diver in excellent physical condition who has been diving actively for at least a year following a basic course, and who has been diving recently in the waters off California. We consider an *advanced* diver to be someone who has completed an advanced certification diving course, has been diving recently in California waters, and is in excellent physical condition.

You will have to decide if you are capable of making any particular dive, depending on your level of training, physical condition, and confidence, as well as the water conditions at the site. Remember, water conditions can change at any time, even during a dive. Know your limitations! The reason for diving is to enjoy and relax. Pushing your limits will certainly lessen your enjoyment of diving and may put you in danger.

If you are only experienced in diving coral reefs or in lakes and quarries, diving the California Channel Islands will be very different and wonderfully unique for you. It is important to adjust slowly to the unusual marine environment that California has to offer. The California marine environment holds many unique habitats that are exciting to explore but can be dangerous if the diver is not informed or trained properly.

Kelp grows in abundance around the Channel Islands. It is home to a great number of marine species. ➤

1

Overview of the Channel Islands

At practically any point along the populous Southern California coastline, were you to head out to sea you would almost certainly run into or pass close to one of the eight California Channel Islands. Each island has its own particular and unique characteristics but at the same time share much in common. The eight Channel Islands can be broken up into two groups of four islands each.

The Northern Channel Islands. These are made up, in an east to west chain, of Anacapa, Santa Cruz, Santa Rosa, and San Miguel islands. They are an offshore extension of the Santa Monica mountains, the mountain range that lies behind the popular Malibu beach area of Los Angeles. This chain of islands is ruggedly spectacular. Much of their shoreline is characterized by sheer cliffs permeated with caves. Arch rocks, pinnacles of volcanic rock, and quiet coves are common. All of these uninhabited islands, along with southern Santa Barbara Island, comprise the Channel Islands National Park.

Southern Channel Islands. This group is made up of, in order of size from the smallest to the largest, Santa Barbara, San Nicolas, San Clemente and Santa Catalina islands. Catalina Island is the only island in all the Channel Islands with a substantial permanent population concentrated in its only town, Avalon. The southern group is much more loosely organized, geographically speaking. Essentially, they are ridges in the sea bottom rising up to break the surface in varying degrees.

History. Before the appearance of the Europeans, almost all of the Channel Islands were inhabited by the Chumash Indians. These inhabitants hunted seals and sea lions, ate abalone and other shellfish and were expert seamen in their sturdy canoes. They were superb craftsmen as well and many artifacts have been collected from the islands and, more recently, from under the water.

The islands were discovered by Europeans in 1542 by Juan Rodriques Cabrillo, believed to be a Portuguese navigator in service to Spain. Cabrillo died from complications of a fall on that journey and is believed to be buried on the island he called *San Lucas* (now San Miguel or possibly Santa Rosa Island) with his jeweled sword reported to be worth over $60,000. The grave site has never been found. Other explorers followed, including Sebastian Vizcaino, Gaspar de Portola, and English Captain George Vancouver, who in 1793 placed the present names of the islands on nautical charts.

The eight Channel Islands lie along the coast of Southern California. They offer a wide variety of diving adventures for the novice to advanced diver. ➤

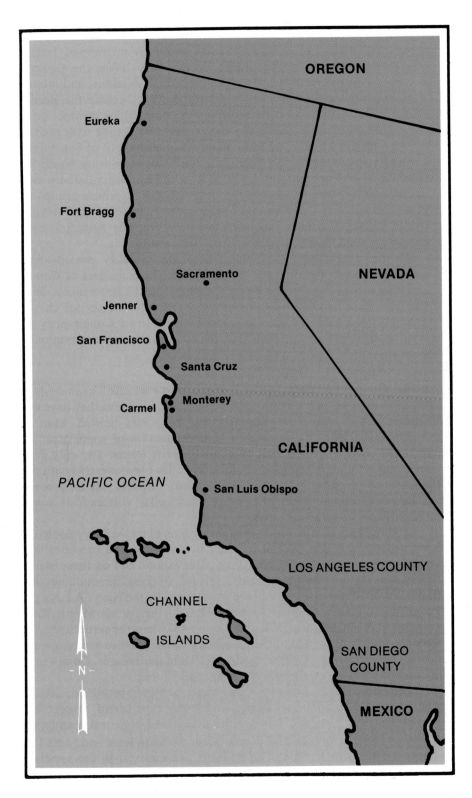

OREGON

Eureka

Fort Bragg

Sacramento

NEVADA

Jenner

San Francisco

Santa Cruz

Carmel

Monterey

CALIFORNIA

PACIFIC OCEAN

San Luis Obispo

LOS ANGELES COUNTY

CHANNEL

ISLANDS

- N -

SAN DIEGO
COUNTY

MEXICO

In the late 18th century and into the 19th century, hunting for sea otter, seals, and sea lions by American, British and Russian trappers brought those species to near extinction. Also, in the early 1800s, the Chumash Indians were moved from the islands to the coastal missions, and hunters, settlers and ranchers moved in. Ranching quickly became the primary economy of the islands with the exception of some fishing camps.

At the turn of the century, the U.S. Coast Guard took over management of Anacapa Island. The U.S. Navy assumed control of San Miguel, San Clemente, and San Nicolas islands in the 1930s and during World War II. In 1938, President Roosevelt declared Anacapa and Santa Barbara as the Channel Islands National Monument. In 1978, due to private groups and cooperation between the National Parks system and the U.S. Navy, the Channel Islands National Park was formed to include Anacapa, Santa Cruz, Santa Rosa, San Miguel and Santa Barbara islands.

Of the eight Channel Islands, these are privately owned—Santa Catalina and Santa Cruz islands. In 1975, over three-quarters of Catalina Island was turned over to the Santa Catalina Island Conservancy, an independent conservation organization, by the Wrigley family (of chewing gum fame). A similar action was taken by the Nature Conservancy that secured a large portion of Santa Cruz Island, assuring its conservation for posterity.

The Channel Islands Today. For the most part, the Channel Islands today are preserved in the same natural rugged condition as they have been for thousands of years. Development has been very limited. Man has brought his influence to the islands with destruction of some plant and animal life and the introduction of non-native life forms. The only developed island is Catalina and much of its growth has been severely restrained. The town of Avalon on the northeast end of Catalina has long been a popular resort among Los Angeles residents as well as visitors from around the country.

Landing, except in an emergency, is prohibited on the Navy-controlled San Clemente and San Nicolas islands. It is not unusual to see military planes, ships and other activities taking place around and on these islands. Because of the military operations, several sections surrounding these islands are off-limits or can be closed as required by the Navy. A large portion of the Northern Channel Islands falls into the Pacific Missile Range and, although not frequently, is also subject to closure or restrictions. The Navy has long used several of the islands for target practice and as a consequence live explosives are still occasionally found underwater. Do not touch any questionable objects in the Navy-controlled areas.

Going ashore is permitted on Catalina (free hiking permit required for back country), Santa Barbara Island, and at Anacapa Island (except West Island other than Frenchy's Cove) without any kind of permit. Landing on San Miguel requires a permit as does landing on Santa Rosa and Santa Cruz islands. Procedures for obtaining permits are outlined in the appendix. Camping, although primitive, is allowed on Anacapa and Santa Barbara

The lighthouse on the San Pedro Breakwater greets many returning happy divers to the mainland. Over ten dive charter boats run out of the Los Angeles/Long Beach Harbor alone.

islands. There are some camping areas on Catalina as well, some of them private.

With the only exception being at Avalon on Catalina Island, going ashore is not the best way to see and dive the islands. Because of the islands' rugged shorelines, and general lack of facilities, a boat is the preferred way to see the Channel Islands. Several dive charter boat operations run out of San Diego, Santa Barbara, the Los Angeles area, and the Ventura area harbors. Many of these dive charter operations are some of the best in the world with comfortable live-aboard accommodations, huge galleys with heaps of gourmet food, and all the facilities a diver may need. Some of these operations specialize in single day trips while others create mini-vacations of two, three, or four days or more that visit and dive nearly all the islands. See the appendix for a complete list of dive boats that service the islands. There is regular ferry service to Avalon, Catalina from San Pedro, Long Beach, Newport Beach and San Diego, where a variety of hotel accommodations can be found. The dive charter boats serve Catalina as well but are able to reach a much larger spectrum of dive sites than what would be available through shore diving.

For those wishing to combine a tour of the mainland with diving, there is a nearly unlimited choice of lodging varying from camping to some of the world's greatest hotels. Shopping and nightlife is also concentrated on the mainland. Los Angeles and all of Southern California is noted as being a party town. All types of food are available in Southern California as well, from Asian to Mexican, from extravagant to dirt cheap. Be sure to try the "California" type of cuisine. Avalon, on Catalina Island, does have its share of good restaurants and night spots but is quiet by mainland standards.

Sightseeing in Southern California at spots other than the islands can fill a lifetime. Some of the main tourist attractions include the beaches, Hollywood, the Mission Trail, Disneyland, and of course, people-watching. Be sure to lock up or otherwise secure your valuables when sightseeing. Crime is not rampant in California but there are criminals.

Getting around in metropolitan Los Angeles and surrounding areas is simple—you need a car. Southern California was built for cars. Freeways seem to come from and go to everywhere and, although they frequently become clogged, are the most efficient way to get around. We suggest that you either bring your own car or rent one. If flying into the area, there are major airports at Los Angeles, Long Beach, San Diego, Newport Beach (Orange County), and Santa Barbara. There is also air service to Catalina Island. Many of the dive charter boats are only a few minutes drive from these airports and taxi service is available.

If you wish to take your own vessel to the islands, there are a few things that you must be made aware of. First, do not try to navigate these waters if you are inexperienced in open ocean travel. The weather in the channels between the islands and the mainland can be unpredictable and change suddenly, particularly in the Northern Channel Islands. Second, obtain good charts. These will help you avoid the hidden hazards common around many of the islands and will steer you clear of restricted areas. And finally, contact the Coast Guard before venturing out as they will inform you on key conditions such as weather and the "LNM," or Local Notice to Mariners, that informs skippers as to military operations and closures as well as other important items. There are boat launching facilities at nearly all of the major harbors but the only island with any kind of provisions or services is Catalina. Boat rentals are scarce and mostly for small coastal boats or sailboats.

Temperature. California may be noted for its sunshine but do not be fooled, it does get cool in California. Along the coast and over the ocean you can expect these general conditions: May thru mid-July, cool overcast skies in the mornings and evenings, highs in high 60s to low 70s, lows into high 50s; July thru October, generally clear days with occasional overcast, highs into the 80s, lows into 60s; November thru April, varied weather including rain, cool clear days and overcast, highs from high 50s up to low 70s, lows into 40s. Regardless of the time of year bring at least a lightweight jacket. Winter will require a heavier jacket, preferably the windbreaker type.

Diving in the Channel Islands offers a variety of marine environments and can be very rewarding.

2

Diving the Channel Islands

Diving the California Channel Islands is a unique and wonderful experience, particularly if you have never dived the California waters before. The waters around these islands are generally cool and clear and are filled with an incredible variety and quantity of sea life.

Visibility. Visibility at the islands is usually very good, averaging between 30 and 60 feet. The clear open ocean water that surrounds most of the islands keeps the water a deep blue color. Some of the islands have better visibility than others. Anacapa, Catalina, Santa Barbara, San Clemente, and San Nicolas islands are generally regarded as the best in terms of water clarity although it depends heavily on the particular dive site. The best times of year for clear water are the months of August thru October or before the seasonal rains. If the rains come late, November and December are good diving months as well. With the right conditions, visibility of over 70 feet is not unusual at the right locations. Water clarity has been reported up to 100 feet. The poorest months for clear water are March thru June because of plankton blooms and storms but even at this time of year it is not hard to find dive spots with visibility of 30 feet or better.

Currents. Much of the clearness of the water is due to the steady ocean currents that bathe the islands year round. Although currents are common at the Channel Islands, most are not strong enough to prevent diving. Finding a dive site that is out of the current is not difficult. Watch the lay of the kelp before diving as it will indicate direction and strength of the current. If the kelp is lying nearly parallel to the bottom, the current may be too strong to dive. Whenever there is a current, or even the possibility of one, use a current line as strong currents sometime come up suddenly. Also, always dive up current as this will allow you to return to the boat with ease.

Water Conditions. The ocean water temperatures of the Channel Islands are cool but not bitterly cold. They will average from the high 60s to the low 70s in the summer and the mid 50s to the low 60s in the winter depending on location. A wetsuit is necessary for all scuba diving. A 1/4-inch-thick suit is generally recommended but you can get by in late summer with a full-length tropical suit in the southernmost islands or for summer snorkeling. A hood is also recommended. Many of the hard-core Channel Island divers are switching to drysuits but these are not necessary.

The thick kelp beds that surround much of the Channel Islands are what give this underwater world its incredible wonderland-like appearance. ➤

Ocean surface conditions off Southern California are generally mild as well with some exceptions. Passages from the mainland to the islands, particularly to San Clemente and Catalina, are usually calm with average seas of 2 to 4 feet. The northern Channel Islands are a bit rougher with frequent high winds causing the seas to white-cap and creating larger swells. San Miguel Island is noted for its rough seas. Occasional winter storms sometimes create huge swells and few vessels travel during these storms. Winds and seas are most commonly out of the west or northwest but storms from other directions are not uncommon. In the summer, hurricanes off Baja California sometimes kick up strong southerly swells. Most of the islands offer diving and anchorage on all sides so that good diving can be had in all but the severest of weather. Because passage to and between the islands can be rough, persons prone to motion sickness should take measures to prevent it.

There is no "typical" diving depths, per se, for diving the Channel Islands. The sea bottom around the Channel Islands is variable. Typical depths of the kelp beds, the most popular diving attraction, are from 20 to 70 feet. There are, however, several popular dive sites that have sheer drop-offs to over 180 feet. The depth ranges that California sport divers most often dive are between 25 and 80 feet. Beyond 70 to 90 feet there is really little else additional to see other than an isolated wreck or two. Typically, the sea bottom around the islands is usually rocky with some large ledges, crevices, and small caves. Larger caves are sometimes found underwater but cave diving is not a normal activity because there is little of interest in these caves and they can be quite dangerous. Interspersed between the rocks are usually patches of sand and the rocks often end in a gently sloping sand bottom at one point or another.

Diving at the Channel Islands is mostly geared toward the scuba diver although snorkelers can find plenty to see and do as well. Casual snorkelers will find the islands of Anacapa and Catalina more to their liking because of their mild conditions and shallower depths. In the town of Avalon on Catalina Island there is an underwater park, Lover's Cove, that is especially for snorkelers (no scuba allowed) where large fish will eat right out of your hands.

Marine Animals. If you are diving California waters for the first time, several life forms may be new and strange to you. Some are dangerous while others are not but can be so if not dealt with properly. You are probably familiar with sea urchins—California has billions of them. They are not poisonous but should you put your hand or knee down in the wrong place you will get stuck, even through a wetsuit or thick gloves. Moray eels in California are not aggressive, however, should you put your hand into a hole before looking, you may stick it right into a moray's mouth and they do have sharp teeth. The scorpionfish (sometimes incorrectly called sculpin) is much like the stonefish with stinging dorsal fin spine but the injury the scorpionfish delivers is more painful than deadly. The torpedo ray is another unusual and dangerous California sea creature to steer clear of.

Lobster are a favorite quarry of those that dive the Channel Islands. Although more abundant on some islands than others, they are a popular, tasty crustacean. Photo by D. Douglass

They are rounded in shape with a tail with rounded fins. They are also called Pacific electric rays and rightfully so. They can be aggressive and will deliver an electric jolt if provoked. California has sharks as does any ocean, the most common being the beautifully graceful blue shark. Those who have been lucky enough to encounter them have got some great photos. Although sharks are common in the open Pacific off California, shark sightings by divers at the Channel Islands are rare but should an encounter occur, treat them with the respect they deserve. Seals pose a greater threat to Channel Island divers than do sharks. Seals and sea lions are plentiful around all the Channel Islands. They are playful and love to tease and dart about divers. Do not, however, attempt to touch them. Although most are quite friendly, some may take your innocent touch as an act of aggression and respond with a deep bite.

Underwater Hunting. If you are coming to the Channel Islands for underwater hunting you are coming to the right place. The California Channel Islands are probably the best underwater hunting grounds in the world. Lobster are common and abalone are not hard to find either. Abalone is a large, meaty mollusk that looks much like a limpet and tastes like heaven. Rock scallops are another favorite and tasty quarry of the local underwater hunters. They are easy to get and easy to prepare. Spearfishermen from the neophyte to the seasoned pro will enjoy the Channel Islands. Relatively easy gamefish are available along with the fish that will challenge any hard-core sportsman.

Underwater hunting in California is, however, strictly governed and regulated to conserve the natural resources. Most all of the common game species have seasons, size limits and bag limits. All game taking requires a valid California Fish and Game license. Pick up a copy of the California fish and game regulations available at many California sporting goods stores.

The best way to explore and dive the Channel Islands is by boat. With the only exception being at Avalon and the Isthmus on Catalina Island, beach diving is non-existent. Southern California has a fleet of over 20 fine dive charter boats ranging from modest to luxurious to serve your diving needs. Many of these boats are fully equipped with hot showers, compressors, and galleys. Trips of one or more days and multi-day trips always include excellent food. The boats and the crews running them are some of

Diving California's kelp beds can be a wonderful underwater experience if kelp is dealt with properly.

the best in the world. They are professionals that know the best dive spots. They are eager to answer any questions and will make a dive trip to the Channel Islands joyful, safe and full of fun.

Dive stores on the mainland in California are another great asset to those wishing to dive the Channel Islands. Most offer full rentals (some renting cameras, underwater video, and underwater vehicles), air fills, classes, repairs, and full equipment lines. They are staffed with courteous professionals that will help you whenever possible or direct you to someone that can. Some will even arrange airport pickup, hotel accommodations and boat reservations if you are traveling from outside Southern California.

Dealing with Kelp

The thick kelp beds that surround much of the Channel Islands are what give this underwater world its incredible wonderland-like appearance. The kelp grows at a very high rate and these submarine forests provide an environment for a huge amount of fish and marine invertebrates. Kelp in itself is not dangerous, it is the diver's ignorance of how to deal with it that can make it dangerous. Kelp is not to be feared.

Perhaps the most important thing to remember about kelp is that it breaks easily. You can even bite through it with ease. There is no reason to become tangled in it but if you should, freeing yourself from it is a simple matter. To prevent entanglement, keep your dive gear as streamlined as possible. Turn fin straps inside along with knives and other straps. Stay close to your buddy who can free you as you swim. In passing through kelp find the natural channels that these forests provide. Do not thrash about or turn suddenly as this will lead to entanglement. Leave enough air to surface free of the kelp. Should you find it necessary to pass through kelp on the surface, do so in a crawling type fashion, pushing the kelp down in front of you. You will be surprised how easy this technique is. But most importantly, do not panic should you become entangled. Simply free yourself slowly and carefully, taking care not to become more entangled. Remember, the kelp cuts and breaks easily.

San Clemente Island

San Clemente Island is the southernmost Channel Island with its southern tip lying only a few miles from the border of Mexican waters. San Clemente Island is noted for its clear waters and colorful marine life. The island is 18 miles long and narrow lying in a northwest to southeast direction. The frontside of the island is long and straight made up of sheer cliffs that drop into the sea. The backside of the island by contrast is rugged and rocky with coves and jagged rocks. From a distance the island is rather featureless with no mountain peaks or large hills.

Because San Clemente is generally rocky in nature and the island receives little rain, the water surrounding the island is very clear and deep blue in color. The frequent currents cleanse the waters as well. Use caution as strong currents are common in some areas.

The U.S. Navy owns and operates the island as a Navy airstrip and target range. Approaching the island within 300 yards or landing is prohibited. The local notice to mariners posts what areas will be closed and when for gunnery practice and other hazardous or restrictive activities. There is one small area on the frontside that is restricted at all times. In many diving areas unexploded shells and other explosives are sometimes found. Do not touch or disturb any questionable object.

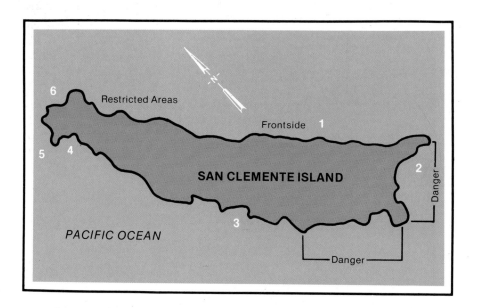

The mostly rocky San Clemente Island is owned and operated by the Navy. About 18 miles long, it lies near the Mexican border. Dive sites of interest include: Frontside (1), Pyramid Head and Pyramid Cove (2), 4½ Fathom Spot (3), West Cove (4), 7-Fathom Spot (5), and the Northwest Harbor wrecks (6).

Transluscent sea squirts frame the soft gorgonian coral in the background.
Photo by Len Tillim.

Typical depth range	:	10 to 50 feet on plateaus, 60 feet and deeper over the drop-off
Typical current conditions	:	Light to moderate
Expertise required	:	Intermediate or better, novice on plateaus with supervision
Access	:	Boat

Most of the frontside (the side facing shore) is sheer cliffs, up to 1000 feet in height, that drop vertically into the sea and continue downward at a steep pace to over 1000 feet in depth less than 1/2 mile from shore. There are, however, several underwater plateaus at several locations along the shoreline. They have been given names by the boat skippers through the years. The most noteworthy for diving are Little Flower, Mosquito Cove, and Wagon Tracks.

Most all of these locations can be found either with a depth finder, visually by way of kelp or, because the water is so clear, by spotting the bottom itself. In most of these locations the underwater plateau slopes gently away from the cliff face from about 10 feet in depth to approximately 40 to 60 feet where the bottom drops away quickly in a series of walls or steep slopes.

The plateaus are made up mostly of large slabs of rock that have fallen away from the cliffs above. Between these rocky reefs are large patches of

Near the edge of the underwater drop that runs along much of the frontside, deep crevices are cut into the rock face.

*A moray eel peeks out of
its lair. Photo by D. Douglass*

clean ivory-colored sand that halibut, angel sharks or huge bat rays often inhabit. Garibaldi seem to love this shallow habitat of rocks, sand patches and kelp. Under many of the slabs, lobster and abalone make their home. San Clemente's frontside is somewhat more often dived so you may have to look a little harder for your game. Try in very shallow, 15 feet or less, for green and black abalone that are sometimes quite abundant.

Skilled spearfishermen have always liked this area for its excellent yellowtail hunting in the summer. Yellowtail are fast pelagic fish that take skill to hunt. Other challenging quarry to be found include the equally fast California barracuda and the shy calico bass. The openwater fish like the barracuda and yellowtail are usually found out near the underwater drop-off.

Near the undersea drop the rocks are sometimes cut with deep channels with rocky walls that contain an abundance of invertebrate life. Reef fish are less common, but there is enough on the crowded rock faces for the photographer and sightseer.

Conditions are generally very good with calm sea conditions prevailing most of the year. Currents can come up but are for the most part weaker than at other locations around the island. Visibility is almost always excellent. The water is a deep blue in color and water clarity of over 60 feet is not unusual. Stay clear of the north end of the lee side, as much of this area is reserved for use by military only.

Typical depth range	:	40 to 80 feet
Typical current conditions	:	Light to moderate
Expertise required	:	Intermediate or better
Access	:	Boat

San Clemente Island has always been a mecca for divers seeking crystal-clear, life-filled waters. It rarely disappoints divers. Visibility at almost all points around the island often exceeds 50 feet, and water clarity of over 80 feet has been reported in some locations. Two of the more probable locations for exceptional visibility are Pyramid Head and Pyramid Cove on the extreme eastern end of the island.

Pyramid Head is not so much a point but more a headland area with a small but very rugged coastal section. The section forms a small cove that is well protected in the prevailing northwesterly weather. This small cove should not be confused with the larger Pyramid Cove to the southwest. Pyramid Cove offers some excellent diving as well.

The shoreline at Pyramid Head is very rugged with many jagged formations of volcanic rock that make up much of the island. Looking at the shore will give you an indication of the bottom formations. The bottom is as rough and varied as the shoreline if not more so. Below the surface of the water you will find reef formations that drop vertically for as much as 60 feet in addition to huge crevices and overhangs. All of this combines with the clear water to make a diver's paradise.

Rugged underwater terrain and spectacular scenery make Pyramid Head a dive spot not to be missed.

Gems like these starfish hide in the rocky bottoms all around the island.

Photographers and sightseers will do exceptionally well here. The patches of kelp are very healthy and create excellent backdrops for photography. Coupled with the clear water, divers seem to float in a mystical forest of blue-green. Brighter colors are there as well. The large ledges support a large number of spectacular red gorgonian. Brightly colored fish, such as garibaldi, sheepshead, treefish, and senoritas swirl about.

Many happy hunters emerge from these waters. Abundant on the reefs are lobster, scallops, game fish, and, to a lesser degree, abalone. Because of the varied bottom, you must look for your quarry in its own particular habitat. Spearfishermen have always liked this spot for its abundant yellowtail, barracuda, and kelp bass.

Due to the clear water and sheer drop-offs, divers are well advised to keep close watch on their depth and pressure gauges. It is easy to forget about depth, bottom time and tank pressure in these beautiful surroundings.

Water and sealife conditions at both sites are very similar but without the radical drop-offs that are sometimes present at Pyramid Head. At this cove the rock and sand bottom drops off at a moderate pace from 30 to 60 feet. Much of the cove is filled with thick, lush healthy kelp. In the center of the cove is an underwater pinnacle known as Cathedral Rock. Photographers and hunters will enjoy this location for its colors and teeming life.

The Navy frequently uses Pyramid Cove for target practice and can close it from time to time. Unexploded shells can sometimes be found underwater—never touch any unusual object.

Also be aware of the current conditions. Observe the lay of the kelp or current line before entering the water and always dive up current. San Clemente Island can be notorious for heavy currents.

Typical depth range	:	30 to 90 feet
Typical current conditions	:	Moderate, some surge
Expertise required	:	Intermediate or better
Access	:	Boat

The southwest or backside of San Clemente is varied and rocky, spotted with points and reefs. Along this side, approximately in the center of the island is a small rocky peninsula called Eel Point. On the north shore of the point lies the broken remains of the wreck *White Eagle*. The bottom drops off to 40 feet directly in front of the point and about 800 yards offshore rises to within 4-1/2 fathoms (27 feet) of the surface; hence the name— 4-1/2 Fathom Spot.

Seaward the reef drops off rapidly to 80 or 90 feet and deeper. The reef is made up of large rock shelves cut by deep channels. There are vertical walls, overhangs and crevices. Breaking up the varied bottom are small patches of white sand.

The rocks are covered with blade kelp and giant kelp. Deeper, the sur-

The varied and rocky terrain of 4½-Fathom Spot is a prime area for underwater photographers and hunters. Marine life in this area hides in the crevices and large rock shelves.

face of the reefs support a variety of invertebrates. The beautiful, rare purple California hydrocoral has reportedly been seen on the deeper ledges. However, the amount of sealife of interest to the photographer is less than at other island locations. The photographer would do best concentrating on the wide variety of fish life that inhabits this reef.

This is prime territory for the hunter. The island backside is the less frequently dove area of the island, making game abundant and accessible. At the 4-1/2 Fathom Spot, abalone and lobster can be found inhabiting this reef. For the spearfisherman, there are kelp bass and sheepshead in large numbers. Other species such as yellowtail and halibut occasionally frequent the area.

Much of the shoreline to the east is similar to this spot, rugged and rocky. Many reefs are marked by kelp beds and are good hunting grounds for lobster and abalone as well as good photo territory. Some of the good points for diving are Mail Point, Lost Point, and China Point.

This particular side of the island is open to the weather and swells from the Pacific, which can be large at times. When approach and anchorage is possible, conditions on the reef are generally good. Visibility averages 30 to 50 feet and currents are common but usually mild. Even small swells can cause surge conditions on the shallower parts of the reef.

The orange and blue Spanish shawl nudibranch is perhaps the most colorful, and common, of all the nudibranchs found in the Channel Islands.

Typical depth range	:	30 to 100 feet
Typical current conditions	:	Light to moderate, strong near the point, some surge
Expertise required	:	Intermediate or better
Access	:	Boat

Most of the backside of San Clemente Island is not divable a good portion of the year due to more exposure to the weather. Because of this, there is less diver pressure to the underwater game on the backside of San Clemente Island and so, lobster, abalone, and other game are relatively abundant. West Cove on the north end is somewhat protected from the prevailing northwest weather, making it a good choice as a consistent game-producing dive location.

Cortez Banks

The most remote and untouched dive spot off the coast of Southern California is Cortez Banks. It is easy to understand why. The banks lie in open ocean over 40 miles from San Clemente Island and nearly 90 miles from the mainland. There are strong currents and deep water. Only the divers experienced in this type of diving should try it but diving Cortez Banks can be a very rewarding dive indeed. The banks are a rise in the sea bottom with two main sections: the 9 Fathom Spot and Bishop Rock. Bishop Rock comes to within only a few feet of the surface and breaks in the swells. Photography, hunting and exploring are exciting in open ocean environments. Lobster are more plentiful here than at any other point in the islands. It is not uncommon to see open ocean variety of fish. Tanner Bank is closer to the mainland with the top reaching about 54 feet. Diving conditions are similar to Cortez Banks. Boat skippers going to the banks must be very experienced in the area.

Kelp at West Cove is anchored in deep, low-lying reefs up to 100 feet deep. Expect to find lobster, abalone, kelp bass and rockfish.

Kelp extends into water nearly 100 feet deep (normal range is 40 to 60 feet) in this area. The kelp is anchored in a bottom that is comprised mostly of low-lying reefs with a great deal of sand between. Many of the reefs have low overhangs and small ridges creating a good environment for lobster and some abalone. The bottom's slope is fairly gentle when compared to the rest of the island.

Gamefish in this area include kelp bass, rockfish in the deeper areas, and occasionally lingcod. Over the sand is a good place to look for large halibut.

Conditions at the cove are variable. Protected from the prevailing northwesterly weather, it is usually a good place to anchor. However, when the swells are coming in, there will be breakers out as far as 200 yards off the west point and considerable surge on the bottom. Visibility is good, averaging 35 to 60 feet. Currents are present but usually weak compared to other locations on the island. Watch for currents off the west point.

Typical depth range	:	50 to 80 feet
Typical current conditions	:	Moderate to strong
Expertise required	:	Intermediate or better, current experience needed
Access	:	Boat

For possibly the clearest, most life-filled waters surrounding San Clemente or any of the Channel Islands for that matter, one needs to dive the underwater mount known as 7-Fathom Spot. The 7-Fathom Spot lies less than a mile west-northwest from Castle Rock at the extreme western end of the island. The rocky bottom comes to within 42 feet of the surface and is an irregular set of ledges, boulders and crevices that drops quickly in some places and moderately in others. Most of the diving depths range from 50 to 80 feet.

On and around the rocks are a large population of fish including garibaldi, a number of types of rockfish, the yellow and black striped tree fish or convict fish, and many other colorful small species that make for interesting photography. Fish for the hunter include large sheepshead, calico bass, and sometimes yellowtail. Hiding among the rocks are lobster and abalone.

Castle Rock, in toward shore, holds much of the same underwater conditions—clear water and abundant life. Castle Rock (also known as Target Rock) has been used by the Navy for target practice over the years and consequently unexploded shells may still be found on the bottom surrounding the rock. Never touch any questionable object.

Rare and beautiful purple coral can be found at both spots. On the inside of Castle Rock, this normally deep-water gem can be found in water as shallow as 35 feet. Although specimen-taking is not prohibited, it is good conservation to leave this rarity alone for others to enjoy. Purple coral take decades to grow only a few inches.

Castle Rock is believed to be the remains of an old volcanic crater that spawned the islands long before man. The best diving at the rock is on the inside between the island and the rock in depths of 30 to 40 feet. On the outside of the rock the bottom drops quickly and currents can be very intense.

Both of these locations tend to be for the experienced diver as they are open to the weather and strong currents are common. An experienced skipper is needed to locate the 7-Fathom Spot and anchor at both locations.

Typical depth range	:	25 to 80 feet
Typical current conditions	:	Light to moderate, surge in shallow
Expertise required	:	Intermediate or better
Access	:	Boat

San Clemente Island, dominated by the U.S. Navy since the 1930s, has long been a favorite target practice area. Not content with just shooting at the Island and surrounding rocks, the Navy occasionally would use target vessels for such practice. The artillery practice and busy naval activities have left the Northwest Harbor section of San Clemente Island with more than its share of sunken shipwrecks.

The most noteworthy of these wrecks is the destroyer escort *John Butler*. The 308-foot vessel saw a great deal of action in World War II and Korean War but was destined to become a target for Navy artillery off San Clemente Island in the early '70s. Eventually sunk, the remains of the bow were removed to deeper water while the stern remains in the harbor 70 feet below the surface. It is possible to enter the wreck from the mid-section. Use caution because although the hatchways have been removed, there is still considerable fouling material inside. The outside decks are a cornu-copia of marine life.

In only 25 feet of water or less, off the eastern tip of the harbor, is an old tugboat. The *Koka* ran aground here in 1937. Abandoned, she eventual-ly broke up and is now little more than rubble on the bottom.

A diver cruises over the depth charge racks on the wreck of the John Butler. *Photo by D. Douglass*

Santa Catalina Island

Santa Catalina Island, which is located only 18 miles (at the nearest point) from the coast, is the most popular of all the Channel Islands. Many people feel that this is the most beautiful of all the islands. Its rolling mountains are sprinkled with green trees, and in wet months the island shines like an emerald on the sea.

The town of Avalon, situated on the lee (shoreward) side of the east end of the island, constantly draws tourists from all over the country and the world. Access is made easy by the regularly scheduled ferry service from the mainland. Regular air service is also available. Avalon is small, relaxed, and peaceful. It offers fine restaurants and shopping along the town's waterfront. Beach diving is only a short walk away.

Catalina is one of the largest of the Channel Islands and the only one with a substantial permanent population. The island runs, approximately, from east to west. It is a little more than 18 miles long, 8 miles across at the widest point, and only one-quarter mile across at the Isthmus. The shoreline is varied, with small sandy coves, sheer cliffs, and rocky beaches. Catalina has a terrain of rolling mountains with some of the highest peaks of all the islands. On moderately clear days, the island is easily visible from the mainland.

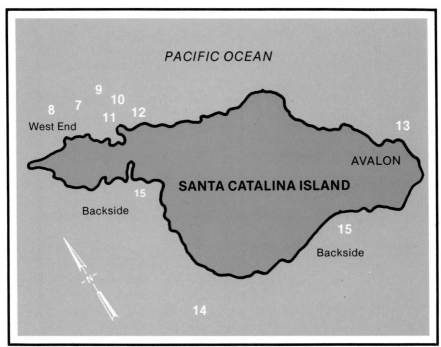

Santa Catalina is the most popular of all the Channel Islands. It is more populated than the others, and the terrain includes sandy beaches, cliffs, and rolling mountainsides. Dive sites include: Eagle Reef (7), West End (8), Ship Rock (9), Bird Rock (10), Isthmus Reef (11), Blue Caverns (12), Avalon (13), Farnsworth Bank (14), and Backside (15).

Colorful gorgonians are made of tiny polyps, each a unique, single, living organism. Similar to the sea fan, these organisms, or cnidarians, are less brittle.

Catalina is one of the few islands on which you may roam about with relative freedom (only a hiking permit is required). Bison (buffalo) roam free, along with goats, deer, and wild pigs brought to the island long ago by man.

The island has some of the clearest, most life-filled waters of any in the islands. Although much diving is done here, it still retains much of its underwater beauty. Most of the diving is concentrated on the frontside or lee of the island where calm ocean conditions prevail much of the year. (Shore access is very poor in all areas other than Avalon and the Isthmus.) A wide range of diving interests can be satisfied here because the sea bottom holds shallow reefs, drop-offs, and lush kelp beds all within a few miles of each other.

The water temperatures at Catalina are considered subtropical. During the late summer, surface water temperatures into the 70s are not unusual. Snorkeling or even shallow scuba diving can be done in a full-length tropical suit, although most local divers still prefer a full 1/4-inch suit. Subtropical fish like the waters as well. The colorful orange garibaldi is the most common fish at Catalina. Small and richly colored blue-banded gobies also enjoy the warmer waters, darting about small cracks in rocks.

Typical depth range	:	30 to 90 feet
Typical current conditions	:	Moderate to strong
Expertise required	:	Intermediate
Access	:	Boat

One of Catalina's largest and most healthy kelp beds lies on the reef known as Eagle Reef. The reef is about 600 yards from shore just west of Isthmus Cove and is marked by a single buoy. The bottom is made up of three mounts. The easternmost, where the buoy is located, comes to within 35 feet of the surface. Little kelp grows at this location. The middle rise comes to within just a few feet of the surface, and at the western end of the reef the rocks reach within 10 feet of the surface. Most of the reef averages in depth from 30 to 60 feet. Steep drops on both sides reach to a sand bottom at 90 feet on the shore side and at over 100 feet on the seaward side. The reef itself is a conglomeration of bedrock, larger boulders, smaller rocks and

Encrusting sponges are found on the undersides of ledges in current-swept areas of the Channel Islands.

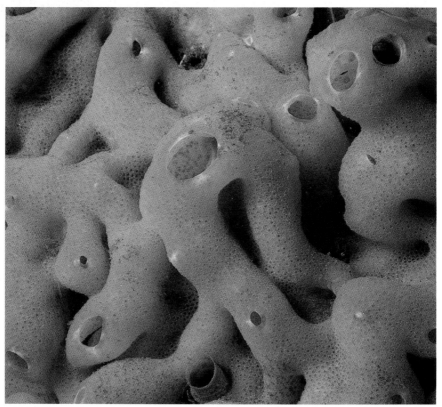

Eagle Reef is plagued with strong currents but these currents bring fantastic visibility and colorful sea life.

patches of sand. A number of crevices and overhangs provide for interesting exploration.

The photographer will enjoy the clear waters, which make an excellent backdrop for photographing colorful invertebrates that are common on the reef. Colorful starfish, colonies of brightly colored anemones, and blue and orange Spanish shawl nudibranchs are not difficult to find. The fish are a wonder to watch. Large and friendly orange garibaldi are present, along with an unusual number of juvenile sheepshead.

The underwater hunter will find good spearfishing opportunities—among the available species are the calico bass, the sheepshead and, even occasionally, the white sea bass or the yellowtail. Lobster can also be captured here. Although somewhat less common, abalone and rock scallops can also be taken.

This dive spot tends to be more for the diver with some experience because of its open location. Strong currents can occur suddenly and boat traffic can be heavy.

The shoreline in this area provides some excellent and slightly more tame diving but falls within a protected zone from Arrow Point to Lionhead Point. No invertebrates can be taken within this zone.

Typical depth range	:	20 to 60 feet
Typical current conditions	:	Moderate to heavy, surge
Expertise required	:	Intermediate to advanced
Access	:	Boat

Less diving occurs in the West End than in any other frontside section of Catalina. Consequently, most types of game there abound. Lobster is not abundant, but it can usually be found. Abalone is fairly easy to find. Spearfishermen like this area for the unusually large sheepshead and halibut.

Diving depths range from 20 to 60 feet. The bottom terrain is generally one of boulders and rock separated by patches of sand. There is a sand bottom further out in deeper water. Kelp patches are easy to find close to shore, and a large quantity and variety of sea life can be found among them.

The West End is somewhat more exposed to the ocean conditions. Much of the area is plagued by currents and, on the extreme West End in particular, heavy seas. The water is generally very clear and provides excellent photographic opportunities.

Colorful Catalina diving can also be done on the west end of the island.

Typical depth range	:	20 to over 150 feet, depending on location
Typical current conditions	:	Moderate to strong, surge in shallows
Expertise required	:	Intermediate to advanced
Access	:	Boat

Ship Rock is a 75-foot-high pinnacle off shore from the Isthmus. It drops rapidly underwater to a series of cliffs and plateaus over 150 feet in height. There is heavy kelp in some sections with large pieces of the rock broken from the main rock. This is described by some divers as the most spectacular dive spot on the entire front side of the island.

Water around this rock is incredibly clear, with excellent visibility. Heavy ocean currents can plague the rock at times but diving in the lee of the current will help. Although the front side of Catalina is noted for its calm water, Ship Rock is far enough out from the island that the seas can be rough. Surge is sometimes a problem in the shallow sections. Much of the diving conditions and bottom configuration depends on what side of the rock you choose to dive.

Photography and spearfishing are excellent on all sides because of the large variety and quantity of fish available. Rockfish and sheepshead are always plentiful. White sea bass have been seen in the deeper sections, and hunters will also find lobster in some locations. The diverse array of subject matter creates superb photographic opportunities. Morays, colorful anemones, and gorgonians are some good examples of possible subjects.

One of the more abundant creatures on the reefs at the Channel Islands is the giant keyhole limpet. Some divers use this mollusk as a substitute for abalone.

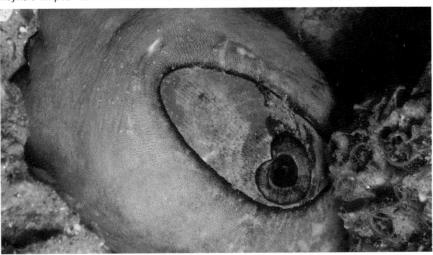

Typical depth range	:	20 to 80 feet, east side drops quickly to 190 feet
Typical current conditions	:	Moderate to strong tidal currents
Expertise required	:	Intermediate to advanced, novice with supervision
Access	:	Boat

Bird Rock sits at the entrance to Isthmus Cove on the front side of Catalina. There is, quite frankly, not much to look at from the surface. It is a large mound-shaped rock covered with bird droppings that give it an almost ice-white appearance. With the exception of the many birds and their droppings, little else other than a few cacti survive on the rock. However, below the surface of the water is another story.

The sea bottom around Bird Rock is varied, with boulders, canyons, cliffs, drop-offs, crevices, and plateaus. Bird Rock is one of the Catalina sites most frequently chosen by divers, yet it still retains much of its underwater beauty and game. It's easy to understand why this has always been a very popular spot with sport divers.

Most boats prefer to anchor on the west or southwest side of the rock. Here, the bottom drops off gently to a rocky plateau varying in depths from 15 to 30 feet. This is an excellent area for snorkeling. Further out, crevices and canyons are interspersed with limited kelp growth, creating interesting diving in deeper waters of 40 to 50 feet. The bottom turns to sand at 50 to 60 feet in this area.

On the northeast side of the small island, the rocky bottom drops off in sheer cliffs to well over 120 feet. Anchorage is difficult here and best avoided. For diving on interesting cliffs and ledges, most divers stay toward the north and west ends.

Bird Rock, a featureless round mound at the mouth of Isthmus Cove, gets its white color from the layers of bird droppings left over the years.

Almost all levels of divers will enjoy the clear, calm waters of Isthmus Reef and Bird Rock.

The entire underwater area is excellent for photography and sightseeing. Visibility around the rock is seldom less than 30 feet and often more than 60 feet. The varied bottom offers an excellent variety for the photographer. The underwater cliffs and ledges frequently have strands of beautiful gorgonians. The sparse kelp to the south and east also make excellent subjects, filtering the light from above through their stalks.

On the bottom and in the surrounding waters are delightful animals. Seals are common visitors. Garibaldi, senoritas, kelp fish, and colorful blue-banded gobies are just a few of the fish species. Large electric, or torpedo, rays sometimes cruise the reefs. They can be interesting but steer clear because they can be dangerously aggressive. Invertebrates include nudibranchs, urchins, a variety of colorful starfish, and other less attractive blobs like sea cucumbers, keyhole limpets and sea hares.

Considering the large amount of diving that occurs in this area, it is still a good spot for underwater hunting. Finding just the right hole or cave can yield several lobster. Abalone are also still available on the rocks, including the rare white, or Sorenson, abalone, the most tender and tasty of all the abalone family. This animal likes deeper water but can occasionally be found in as little as 40 feet on the west side. Pay attention to your calendar when hunting abalone on this side of the island because the season is shorter (April 1 to October 1).

Spearfishermen sometimes still bag white sea bass at this location, but this species is becoming less common. Kelp bass, sheepshead and sometimes halibut are common game.

Conditions at the rock are generally good, but beware of strong currents particularly during times of tidal changes. Anchor and dive close to the rock as the Isthmus Harbor can, at times, be subject to a great deal of boat traffic.

Typical depth range	:	25 feet to 80 feet, some sections deeper
Typical current conditions	:	None to light
Expertise required	:	Novice to intermediate
Access	:	Boat

Isthmus Reef (sometimes called Harbor Reef) lies almost directly in the middle of Isthmus Cove and covers several acres. The reef breaks the surface at one point during low tide. Most of the reef lies in 30 to 40 feet of water but drops sharply to 80 to 120 feet in some places, creating walls, crevices and caves filled with marine life.

The sharpest drop-off is on the north and east sides. The walls of rock are a habitat for colorful gorgonia, anemones and other invertebrates. Other colorful critters inhabiting the rocks include the red and blue striped tiny blue-banded goby. Garibaldi are common all over the island and always make excellent photo subjects because of their bright orange color. The walls on the entire reef make an excellent backdrop for photographers.

Conditions on the reef are usually quite good. The reef is removed from the rest of the island, making it open to cleansing currents that keep

Horn sharks are very abundant in some locations at Catalina. These sharks are, for the most part, harmless. Reaching over four feet in length, they can be a handful if you choose to do some shark wrestling. Most, however, are less than two feet long.

Urchins are very abundant throughout California. Although not poisonous, some of their spines are needle sharp and can penetrate wetsuits and gloves. Always use caution in where you place your hands and knees.

the water very clean. Visibility averages 50 feet but can exceed 100 feet. In addition, the reef lies within a cove protected on three sides. The waters here are calm most of the time.

At one time, kelp covered the reef in heavy beds. Presently the kelp is thin and patchy. The kelp will most likely return some day soon, but for now the reef is open and unencumbered.

Much game still lives on and around the reef, considering the heavy diving activities in the last several years. Lobster, sometimes in large numbers, can be found in caves and crevices in the drop-off areas. These are smart bugs seasoned by years of intrusive divers, so approach quietly if you want to get close. The larger game fish are not in residence, but kelp bass and sheepshead are common. Halibut can sometimes be found in the sand surrounding the reef edges.

Perhaps what makes this dive site so attractive is its versatility. Beginning divers will find excellent diving within their limitations on top of the reef, whereas more experienced divers can descend the drop-offs to more challenging diving and decide on their own limitations. Hunters and photographers will also find plenty to delight in. And finally, with the large size of the reef, you can dive with a charter boat full of divers and still not come across another group.

On the shoreline near the cove diving is excellent. Big Fisherman Cove, directly to the east, is a favorite spot. The buildings on shore house a diver recompression chamber and the USC Marine Science Center.

Typical depth range	:	30 to 90 feet
Typical current conditions	:	Moderate to strong
Expertise required	:	Intermediate to advanced
Access	:	Boat

For sightseeing, adventure and just the thrill of diving, Blue Caverns on Santa Catalina Island is not to be missed. Blue Caverns offers cave diving, wall diving, and excellent photography all within a small stretch of island.

Blue Cavern Point is an extension of volcanic rock on the front side of Catalina that marks the eastern edge of Isthmus Cove. Within this lava rock are two caves that are particularly notable. Perdition Cave and spouting Cave extend as much as 150 feet into the island. Small boats and inflatables can be driven into them. The surrounding cliffs and rocks hold a number of smaller caves, some of which are only visible under water. At some points, the cliffs drop directly into the sea, straight down to as much as 90 feet.

What truly holds the eye of the diver in this area are the spectacular strands of gorgonia, sponges, and corynactis anemones. There is color everywhere you turn because many of the "wall" areas are covered with this growth. A steady and prolific current feeds these plankton eaters. The spectacular array of sea life does not end there. Depending on what particular

Green abalone are common in the shallow sections of Catalina.

At Blue Caverns, steep slopes of jumbled rock hide the mottled red and gray fragile stars.

section of the reef you are at, you can expect to see numerous nudibranchs, moray eels, the gray and red fragile star, and the bright orange blood star. Healthy kelp spots the area, supporting an abundant fish population. Fish in the rocks include the tiny, but intensely colorful, blue-banded goby or striped zebra goby. Yellow and black striped treefish hide in some of the larger cracks. All in all, Blue Caverns is perhaps the most colorful of the dive sites on the front side of Catalina Island.

Hunters should just enjoy the scenery. The point is poor on lobster and game fish but scallops can sometimes be found. Occasionally pelagic fish such as yellowtail or white sea bass will cruise past the point.

Visibility at the point and around the caves is a minimum of 40 feet. It can reach 100 feet at times. Currents keep the water clear of debris. You can expect a minimum current of 1/2 to 1 knot, and depending on tides and conditions, currents can often exceed 3 knots. These currents can be tricky and hazardous, particularly in the caves, so use caution. The strong currents can sometimes be avoided by diving east toward the rock quarry. The currents and the depths make this a spot for the intermediate or advanced diver. On the lee side of the island, swells and surge are rarely a problem except with a Santa Ana wind condition.

Because of the currents and deep water, anchorage can be difficult. If you plan to take a private boat to the location, be sure someone on board has experience in anchoring under such conditions. It is also a good idea to carry a secondary anchor for anchoring the stern of the boat.

Typical depth range	:	20 to 90 feet
Typical current conditions	:	None to light
Expertise required	:	Novice to intermediate
Access	:	Beach

Avalon has the charm of a Mediterranean island village, the homey quality of an American town, and top quality diving that is often only a few steps away from hotels and transportation. Avalon is the only place in the Channel Islands where one can effectively make beach dives. The two main beach diving areas in the town of Avalon are Lover's Cove and Avalon's Underwater Park at Casino Point.

Lover's Cove off the east side of Avalon Bay is a popular area in Avalon. The area is a reserve where no animal or plant life can be removed and only snorkeling is allowed. Sorry, no scuba diving. The cove, however, lends itself well to leisurely snorkeling to explore the rocks, kelp and sand. Most of the sea bottom inside the reserve is less than 30 feet deep. With visibility usually over 20 feet, you can see a great deal by just floating about.

Because it is a reserve, no spearfishing is allowed. Many of the fish are hand-fed by the tourists daily. Consequently, the fish within the cove are very friendly and fat. It is quite a thrill to hand-feed many local varieties of fish that are often impossible to approach at other sections of the islands. At times the fish will swarm around divers if they see or sense food.

The small gravel beach at Lover's Cove is located only a few steps to the east of the ferry landing. The water at the cove is usually dead calm with little or no current, and water entry is very easy. Lover's Cove is an excellent spot to break in a beginner to the underwater world of the Channel Islands.

Directly across the bay is the most recognizable landmark in Avalon: the red-roofed Casino located at Casino Point. Along the seaward side of the point and groin (small breakwater) is the Avalon Underwater Park. The park is cordoned off from boat traffic by buoys and rope, reserving the area for divers.

For traveling divers wishing to get a sample of what the Channel Islands has to offer, the Underwater Park is probably the best location. The park has practically everything: wrecks, drop-offs, pinnacles, kelp beds, and a lot of sea life. What it does not have, however, is game hunting. The park is a reserve and the taking of any kind of game is prohibited.

The wrecks alone are reason enough to dive here. The most noteworthy is the wreck of a 60 ferro-cement sailboat called the *Sue Jaq*.The wreck lies on the seaward side of the extreme eastern corner of the park. The stern is in 60 feet of water and the bow in 95 feet. The sailboat is lying on its side with the bow and stern hatches open. There is also a gaping hole in its side. Divers can see most of the wreck without going below 80 feet. Working westward along the seaward boundary of the park, at a depth of about 60 to 70 feet, you will encounter other fairly recent small wrecks. Up the slope and further to the west is the wreck of a car and the remains of an old pier.

For those wishing to explore kelp, there is a large bed in the center of the park. There are also sharp underwater drop-offs that are thrilling to explore. They drop as much as 40 feet straight down.

Living in and on these underwater features is a multitude of fish and invertebrates. Moray eels are common, the biggest living under the stern of the *Sue Jaq*. The tame and colorful fish against the normally clear waters make for excellent photography.

Coupled with the excellent visibility that averages 40 feet, the calm seas make this an easy dive spot. Currents are weak and infrequent. The only real hazards are the boat traffic just outside the park boundaries and the steep drops to deep water on the east end of the park. Water entry over the rocks can be a little tough.

To the northwest of the park is Descanso Bay. In the middle of the bay in 65 to 100 feet of water is the wreck of a luxury yacht, *Valiant*, which burned and sank in 1932 with a reported $67,000 in jewelry on board that has never been found. Diving this fascinating wreck requires a permit from the harbor office and can only be done by boat. A professional guide or dive charter boat is recommended.

Services in Avalon make diving the park easy. During summer weekends there is a portable air fill station on the point. There are several dive shops in Avalon that rent tanks and other gear and give air fills year round. Getting around Avalon can be done mostly on foot, as everything is close, but divers might consider hiring a taxi or using a hand cart, which can be rented at the dive shop on the pleasure pier in the middle of the bay. There are also lockers available at several locations for those wishing to stow gear.

The most recognizable landmark as you approach the town of Avalon is the red-roofed Casino on Casino Point. Just off the Casino Point breakwater is the Avalon Underwater Park.

Typical depth range	:	60 to 160 feet with drops to 200 feet
Typical current conditions	:	Moderate to strong
Expertise required	:	Advanced, intermediate with supervision
Access	:	Boat

Farnsworth Bank is an undersea pinnacle that rises to within 54 feet of the surface, about 1-1/2 miles southeast of Ben Weston Point on the back side of Catalina Island. The mountain is in crystal blue open ocean water and is surrounded by and overgrown with a huge variety of colorful and interesting marine life.

Gorgonians and anemones are perhaps the most striking sea life. They are brightly colored and in great quantity. Looking a little closer reveals the rare and beautiful California purple coral, more properly called *hydrocoral*. It ranges from purple to light blue in color, and although it is very rare, it can be found at Farnsworth. Taking this coral or any rock specimen is prohibited.

The spearfishermen will find rockfish and some pelagic varieties, but hunting on the rocks for abalone, scallops and lobster is poor.

Diving at Farnsworth is for the experienced diver. Depths range from 60 to over 160 feet with some steep drop-offs. The open ocean location of the reef makes anchoring difficult, and surge and strong currents are common. Careful dive planning is necessary.

The rare and beautiful California purple coral, or hydrocoral, is common at Farnsworth Bank. All coral is protected by law, and the taking of any coral specimen is prohibited. Photo by D. Douglass

Typical depth range	:	20 to 100 feet, depending on location
Typical current conditions	:	Moderate, strong surge
Expertise required	:	Intermediate to advanced
Access	:	Boat

The back side, or ocean-facing side, of Catalina gets the brunt of many storms as well as the day-to-day pounding of surf. There are good places to dive on the back side, particularly for game, but most divers prefer the front side. Because of the rough conditions visibility can vary by location.

Just around the corner of the east end from Avalon is Church Rock. Church Rock lies on the edge of a zone that often has cloudy water. This zone extends eastward from Church Rock to Ben Weston Point. Day-to-day surf pounding on sand beaches creates the turbid water. Church Rock is usually an incredibly beautiful place to dive, with striking blue waters, but visibility may be only 10 to 20 feet.

Some other noteworthy spots are Salta Verde Point, with good visibility on calm days and lots of game, Little Harbor area, with rugged shoreline and sea bottom, and Catalina Harbor. Catalina Harbor is the back side of Isthmus Cove. The island here is only 1/4-mile wide. Catalina Harbor is the only area on the back side that is protected from the weather. The harbor is frequently crowded with boats on the weekends and is not great for diving. Catalina Head, the high rocky headlands on the west side of the harbor, is better. Lobster, abalone and gamefish can be found here.

Further to the west, coves and rocky bays are numerous. Lobster Bay is popular with divers because of its namesake. Iron Bound Cove is another favorite and is partially protected from bad conditions.

Church Rock is just around the east end of the island from Avalon and can offer spectacular diving in blue waters when the conditions are right.

San Nicolas Island

San Nicolas Island is the most remote of all the Channel Islands, lying some 60 to 70 miles off shore. Being the most remote island, San Nicolas is noted for its abundant game. "Nic," as many local divers call it, has probably produced more big, or "bull," lobster than any other location along the coast of Southern California. Abalone, scallops, and gamefish are abundant as well. Huge sheepshead fish, a favorite quarry of local spearfishermen, are easy shooting at San Nic. Large, tasty rockfish are also common.

San Nicolas Island is shaped much like an elongated football. It is somewhat featureless from a distance, taking on the shape of a rounded mound. The island's terrain is also featureless, with dry barren slopes cut with shallow gullies. The shoreline is rugged, and not as beautiful as many of the other islands. Small cliffs and some stretches of beach surround the island.

The U.S. Navy patrols the island, prohibiting landing and restricting activity in much of the surrounding water. Approaching the island closer than 300 yards is prohibited. Some underwater areas see very few divers per year, and it is here that delicate and shy species of invertebrates and fish can often be seen.

As with San Clemente, the Navy has used San Nicolas for target practice. Do not touch any questionable objects you find underwater as they may be explosives.

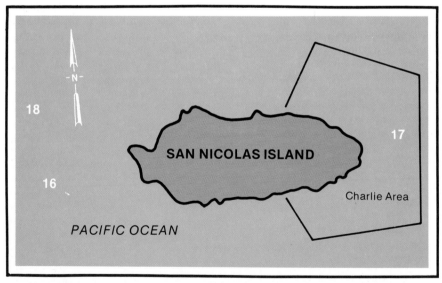

San Nicolas Island is home to many species of game fish and other sea life. Good hunting can be had at The Boiler and 7-Fathom Reef (16). Photography will be best at Charlie Area (17). For a good combination of both hunting and photography, dive at Begg Rock (18).

A close-up of the Corynactis anemone reveals its delicate tentacles. Photo by Len Tillim.

Typical depth range	:	20 to 70 feet
Typical current conditions	:	Moderate, strong surge on shallow boiler
Expertise required	:	Intermediate
Access	:	Boat

Off the west end of San Nicolas Island is a large area of reefs, kelp and water depths that are easily reached by divers. Depths in this area average about 60 feet. The shallowest level at the location is known as "The Boiler." About a mile to the south is the 7-Fathom Reef.

The Boiler is aptly named. The rocks here just barely break the surface, and in the common swells, the sea seems to boil, surging and splashing in a froth of white water. The bottom surrounding the white water is rocky with shelves, boulders and crevices. The bottom drops off at a moderate to gentle pace, making for a wide area of good diving and good hunting.

Hunting is the main reason for coming to The Boiler and 7-Fathom Reef. Lobster and red abalone are the main quarry but large sheepshead, calico bass and scallops are also common.

The photographer will find very clear water and beautiful kelp beds. Invertebrate and other sea life are more abundant in other areas of the island.

Because there is little sand in the area to muddle the waters, visibility is usually very good—on the average 50 feet. The area is, however, subject to surge and currents because of its open location. It is often impossible to anchor nearby and thus very difficult to dive the shallower areas because of the heavy surge.

The lowly purple sea urchin is probably the most abundant of all the sea life around the Channel Islands.

Typical depth range	:	20 to 70 feet
Typical current conditions	:	Weak to moderate
Expertise required	:	Intermediate, novice in some spots
Access	:	Boat

Charlie Area encompasses the eastern third of the island. In most places, the bottom slopes moderately from a depth of 20 feet 300 yards off shore, to 60 and 70 feet at the edge of the kelp beds. The bottom is frequently a series of ledges and reefs. Crevices and holes permeate much of the volcanic rock, and patches of sand are interspersed between the reefs. Perhaps the largest advantage of diving this area is that a diver can stay relatively shallow, 30 to 40 feet, and still enjoy a full range of game and scenic opportunities.

For the sightseer and photographer, San Nicolas seems to be blessed with terrific visibility. The average is between 30 and 40 feet and can occasionally exceed 70 feet. The kelp is thick and healthy. On the rocks, colorful invertebrates can be found, such as a variety of anemones, nudibranchs, and starfish. Schooling fish, such as garibaldi, treefish, gobies, and morays, move about the rocks. An occasional seal may also watch you as you dive.

Hazards are few in this area. The current can be unpredictable, but it is often less strong here than in other parts of the island. Kelp can be thick in spots and kelp diving experience is recommended. Listen to the directions of your captain or divemaster to avoid any trouble. The seas are calmest on the south side. Stay clear of the sand spit on the extreme west end. Anchorage here is prohibited and there is little diving over the sand bottom. However, areas beyond the sand spit can be productive.

The treefish, or convict fish, can be found in rock crevices throughout the Channel Islands. Pictured here is a juvenile measuring only a couple of inches.

Typical depth range	:	Vertical drops to over 250 feet; plateaus and valleys, 120 to 55 feet
Typical current conditions	:	Moderate to strong
Expertise required	:	Advanced, intermediate with supervision
Access	:	Boat

Eight miles off the west end of San Nicolas Island, the undersea pinnacle known as Begg Rock rises 15 feet out of the sea. The automobile-sized monolith appears out of open ocean, almost as if it were floating. Below the water's surface is where Begg Rock inspires awe and wonder.

In several spots around the rock the wall drops vertically to over 250 feet. On the northeast side, there is a plateau at 55 feet with a reported tunnel. In one section, there is a valley that extends from 120 feet up to the main reef. This creates an excellent open ocean environment for a great variety of invertebrates to attach themselves to.

Begg Rock is a macro photographer's dream. Gray moon sponges can be seen here, with a multitude of brittle stars crawling from the sponge's holes. The sponges are pushed for space by the millions of anemones. The assortment of anemones is quite large. Colors range from snow white in the white-plumed anemone (found deeper) to the hot pink of the small strawberry anemone and include many hues of purple and royal blue.

The wide-angle photographer will also do well, for visibility around the rock area is usually 40 feet and has been reported to be as great as 150 feet.

For the hunter there are scallops, in unbelievable quantity and size. You can have your limit of 10 in a matter of minutes, but pick and choose carefully, for you'll want only the largest. Anything smaller than your hand is substandard for Begg Rock. Dinner plate size is not unusual.

Deeper diving hunters will do well on rockfish. Sheepshead are also common in some sections of the rock. Because of the vertical nature of the rock, lobster and abalone are non-existent.

Approach and anchoring on the rock can be very difficult. Because of its open ocean location, seas must be calm. Even so, many dive charter boat captains prefer to live boat or drift dive the rock. Currents can also be a hazard.

Begg Rock is a macro-photographer's dream. The open ocean waters surrounding it support an abundance of colorful anemones. ➤

Santa Barbara Island

The smallest of the Channel Islands is Santa Barbara Island. Little more than a very large rock, this island only covers about 640 acres. The area of diveable water surrounding the island almost exceeds the size of the island itself. The island is triangular in shape and is surrounded on all sides by steep cliffs. Pieces of land surrounding the island include the small Sutil Island and Shag Rock.

Santa Barbara Island is the southernmost island in Channel Islands National Park. One of the two islands of the original Channel Islands National Monument (the other was Anacapa), it is the only island in the present park that is not part of the northern chain of islands. Being part of the National Park, several restrictions apply. The taking of any invertebrates in 20 feet of water or less is prohibited on the entire eastern side of the island. Also, only normal game as per California Fish and Game regulations can be taken around the entire island. As with Anacapa Island, you may land on the island without permission.

Camping is by permit only and limited to a maximum of 30 persons. The facilities on the island are very primitive. There are latrines but no water or trash disposal. You must carry in and take out everything you need over a steep trail leading to the east side landing cove. There are trails for hiking but no access for beach diving.

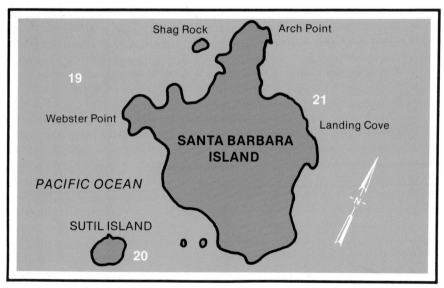

Interesting dive sites surround Santa Barbara Island. Arch Reef and 7½ Spot (19) lies off Webster Point. Sutil Island (20) is a steep rock off the southwest corner of Santa Barbara, and Landing Cove and East Shoreline (21) is located on the northeast tip of the island.

A diver breaks open a sea urchin for a passing garibaldi. These bright orange fish are very popular to the Channel Islands.

Its shores are windswept, for there is not much cover from weather. Much of the island is constantly battered by the seas. Because of this, diving is often confined to deeper (45 feet or more) offshore reefs or the eastern side of the island. Visibility suffers as well. The open ocean waters surrounding Santa Barbara Island are clear, but a nearly constant bottom surge reduces visibility to an average of 30 feet. Some of the offshore locations can, however, have very good visibility. Currents can be strong at times.

Sea life is very abundant. Huge, thick and lush kelp beds surround much of the island. Within the kelp is a cornucopia of fish and animals. On shore, many types of seals and sea lions haul-out. In the water they are very playful, often harassing divers in a dive-bombing technique. They are cute, but do not touch them. They can deliver a nasty bite.

Typical depth range	:	50 to 80 feet
Typical current conditions	:	Moderate, some surge
Expertise required	:	Intermediate to advanced
Access	:	Boat

Off Webster Point on the western end of Santa Barbara Island and extending out over a mile is a large area of rocky, kelp-covered sea bottom. It is within diving depths of 80 feet. The most notable points are Arch Reef and the 7-1/2 Spot.

Arch Reef rises to just below the surface and will break in moderate swell. The reef gets its name from the large underwater arch. The rock drops sharply to 50 or 60 feet on the island side and over 100 feet on the seaward side. The water here is very clear, possibly the clearest on the island. There is an interesting array of life on and around the arch. Rare purple coral has been reported on the rock at fairly shallow depths.

Arch Rock can be very dangerous to approach, as it is concealed in the water when the water is calm. However, seas on this side of the island are often rough, which can put a damper on any boating activity.

Nine hundred yards north of Arch Reef is a rise in the rocky bottom known as 7-1/2 Spot. Its name refers to the depth of its shallowest point, 7-1/2 fathoms (about 45 feet). The area east of the 7-1/2 Spot is a large plateau with an average depth of 60-90 feet. On the plateau and toward shore is a series of sharp underwater pinnacles rising from the bottom as much as 50 feet. In the plateau are large dips or "potholes" averaging 6 feet deep. These holes are a popular hiding place for lobster.

Dives in this area are very rewarding but can be challenging. The often rough seas, bottom surge and depths limit diving to the intermediate and experienced divers.

The giant-spined starfish is one of the largest starfish. This one makes Arch Reef its home.

Typical depth range	:	30 to 120 feet
Typical current conditions	:	Moderate, some strong surge
Expertise required	:	Intermediate to advanced
Access	:	Boat

A section of Santa Barbara lies off the southwest corner. The steep rock is known as Sutil Island.

The small island is surrounded nearly on all sides by healthy kelp. Below the surface, the kelp attaches itself to a variety of terrain.

On the northwest side is a hand-shaped reef that drops off gradually to 60 feet, and then more rapidly to 120 feet. On the weather or north side of the large rock, the bottom drops off quickly. The area between Sutil and Santa Barbara Island is thick with kelp and about 30 feet deep on a rock bottom.

Depending on the section of the island in which you dive, you can find colorful gorgonians, thick beds of anemones, nudibranchs, starfish, and exotic and unusual varieties of sea shells.

The waters surrounding Sutil are clear, averaging 30 to 40 feet of visibility. Because Sutil is open to various weather conditions, other sections of Santa Barbara Island may be clearer. Surge and strong currents can also be a problem. The southeast side is the most protected. An experienced skipper can anchor you in calm and productive locations.

Hunters will find the southwest and northwest sides to be best. The side facing the island tends to have an unproductive bottom. Green, pink and a few red abalone are found to 35 feet deep. Lobsters are found in some of the rock piles and ledges around the island.

Deeper ledges and drop-offs around the small Sutil Island support the beautiful red gorgonian.

Typical depth range	:	20 to 50 near shore, 60 to 90 on offshore plateau
Typical current conditions	:	Light near shore with surge, moderate at plateau
Expertise required	:	Intermediate to advanced
Access	:	Boat

North of Landing Cove on Santa Barbara Island is a series of low lying reefs in shallow water covered with kelp. The rocks end in about 30 feet of water as the bottom turns to gently sloping sand. On shore a large population of pinnipeds (seals and sea lions) often "haul-out" or go ashore. The surrounding kelp beds are their playground and divers often have close contact with these graceful beasts.

A little less than a mile out from the Landing Cove area is a rocky plateau that tops out at 60 feet and runs down to as deep as 90 feet. The plateau is cut with a series of ledges that provide excellent lobster hunting. Spearfishermen will find white sea bass, sheepshead, calico bass and rockfish. Photographers will enjoy the plateau for its clear waters and prolific color. Anemones, nudibranchs and unusual starfish are also common.

In shore, around the landing, the water is not as clear and game is scarce. Remember that the entire side of this island is a reserve, and taking invertebrates in less than 20 feet of water is prohibited. There are animals to see on the shallow rocks, but most divers simply enjoy the antics of the seals. To the south of Landing Cove are several similar reefs, some of which extend into 50 to 60 feet of clearer water.

This is the most protected section of the island and most boats will go here when the wind is blowing strong on the west side. It is, however, not exempt from problems. Swells will cause a surge that can stir up the sand. Near shore, currents are weak, but on the plateau, currents can exist.

Anacapa Island

Anacapa Island is actually three islands divided by narrow straits of impassible water. Anacapa was one of the two original islands (the other being Santa Barbara Island) to make up the Channel Islands National Monument formed in 1938. It was converted to Channel Islands National Park in 1980 with the addition of the three other Northern Islands. Anacapa's three islands are long and narrow, lined up in an east-west chain. The three East and Middle Islands are relatively flat topped. They've been carved down by the ocean during a prehistoric period of higher sea levels. The West Island rises to a single peak of 930 feet. Of all the Channel Islands, Anacapa is the second smallest, yet it is the most spectacular above water. Cliffs, caves, spires of volcanic rocks and a 40-foot-tall arch rock are some of the breathtaking sights around the island. The tall Arch Rock on the extreme east end has become the "trademark" for the Channel Islands National

Anacapa is the second smallest of all the Channel Islands and perhaps the most rugged. Seen here is the view looking at the West End. Cat Rock is to the right.

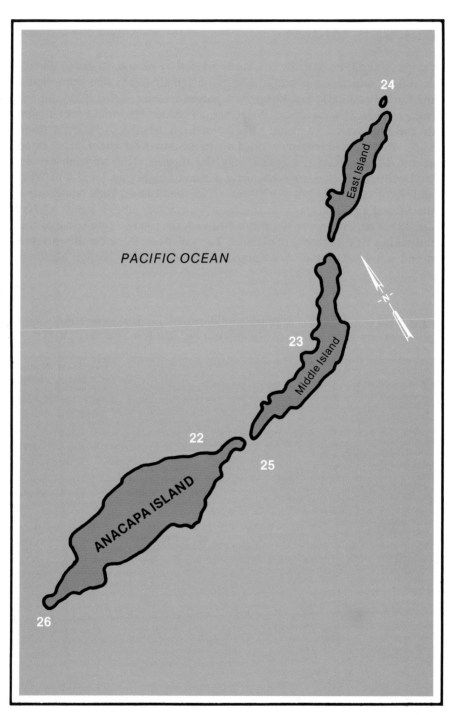

PACIFIC OCEAN

East Island (24)

Middle Island (23)

ANACAPA ISLAND (22) (25) (26)

The three small islands that make up Anacapa are basically flat topped. The island has steep cliffs and the famous Arch Rock (24) at the east end of the island. Other excellent dive sites are Frenchy's Cove and the Pelican nesting area (22), Bat Ray Cove and the wreck of the Winfield Scott *(23), Parallel Reefs (25), and the West End (26).*

Park. A tour around the island is worth a trip in itself. An underwater tour of the island will triple the enjoyment of the visit.

Anacapa is also the closest to the mainland, 11 miles at the closest point. Consequently, it is the most frequently visited of the northern chain. This by no means diminishes its rugged beauty.

The island is rough, rocky and mostly barren. The easternmost island gets the most attention from non-divers. On this section is a picturesque lighthouse, landing cove, a small visitors' center, and primitive camping facilities. Those that wish to land on and explore this rugged terrain will find it is no simple task. The dock at the landing cove is for dinghies only. From the dock, it is only a short distance to the visitors' center. Camping is by reservation only but you must be properly prepared because there is no water or modern toilets. The camps are in the open and subject to seasonal weather and strong winds. For those that truly want to rough it and get a real feel for these rugged islands, this is the way to go. Most who desire to walk on the island do so in one day. Always hike on the designated trails only. There are nature trails and scenic vistas that are breathtaking. After the spring rains, the island comes alive with green grasses and wildflowers.

Landing can also be done without permission on the middle island, but there are no facilities, and there is no access to the top of the island. The West Island is the largest of the three but is closed to the public. It is a sensitive nesting ground for pelicans and other marine birds as well as a hauling-out point for seals and sea lions. Frenchy's Cove is the only exception on the West Island where picnicking is allowed on the small sand beach.

Diving from shore is impossible. For that reason all diving activity is done from boats, either private or one of the many fine dive charter boats that run to the island. There are dive boats running every weekend and several, particularly during the summer, run on weekdays as well. Anacapa is an easy and fulfilling dive trip for one day, but the island holds so many excellent diving areas that one could spend an entire summer of underwater exploration.

Because this is part of the National Park system, there are restrictions to protect the environment that you must be aware of. Everything you bring to the island you must take back with you. There are no trash disposal facilities, and anti-litter laws are strictly enforced. Several underwater areas surrounding Anacapa are restricted as to the type and timing of certain underwater activities. On the entire north side of East Island, the taking or possessing of any type of aquatic life in up to 60 feet of water is not permitted. No invertebrates may be taken in 20 feet of water or less on the southeast end of the West Island, and on most of the north side of the Middle Island. The east end of the West Island and out to a depth of 120 feet is closed to entry from January 1 to October 31 because of nesting pelicans. At Anacapa, and all the Channel Islands falling within the park boundaries, only normal game can be taken as per California Fish and Game regulations in the unrestricted areas. For specifics on all the regulations, request information from the park's main office.

Typical depth range	:	10 to 50 feet
Typical current conditions	:	None to moderate, increasing toward west
Expertise required	:	Intermediate to advanced, novice with supervision
Access	:	Boat

Frenchy's Cove is a small sandy beach at the northeast end of West Anacapa Island. The Cove has good anchorage and excellent shallow snorkeling. Picnicking is allowed on the beach, but overnight camping is prohibited.

West of the Cove is Frenchy's Cave, and a little further down is Indian Water Cave. Both of these large caves provide interesting exploration when the light is right and conditions are good. At Indian Water Cave and to the west to Portuguese Rock is the brown pelican nesting area. The brown pelican is an endangered species and this is the only permanent nesting ground in the United States. The area is restricted to any kind of boat traffic from January 1 to October 31 so not to disturb the nesting pelicans. Except for two months out of the year, November and December, the area is untouched and undisturbed.

This blood star is one of the many living jewels that can be found around the Channel Islands.

This red volcano sponge stands out among the other prolific invertebrate life that lives in the area of Frenchy's Cove.

The sea bottom in this area generally consists of rock and boulders close to shore and then of a moderately sloping sand bottom further out. There is some patch reef further off shore but it usually requires electronics to locate. Depths vary between approximately 10 feet near shore to 30 to 50 feet where the sand bottom begins. Kelp patches are heavy in some areas while other spots are barren.

On the rocks, scallops are numerous but mostly small. Abalone and lobster can also be found, but they are also small. Look close to shore in very shallow water for green and black abalone. Kelp bass and sheepshead are plentiful but spearfishing is discouraged by the National Park Service.

Underwater photographers will find themselves busy with the rocks. There is a wide variety of small colorful fish as well as invertebrates. Blue-banded gobies, gorgonia, and garibaldi are some of the favorite subjects. For unusual subjects, look into the crevices for large octopus or on the sand for an occasional torpedo ray. Playful seals may also frequent this area.

Seas here are generally calm and current-free near Frenchy's Cove, but currents may be strong toward the west. Visibility averages 40 feet or more.

Typical depth range	:	20 to 45 feet
Typical current conditions	:	Light to moderate
Expertise required	:	Intermediate to advanced, novice with supervision
Access	:	Boat

On the northside, along the rugged shoreline of the Middle Island, rocks and spires jut from the shallow waters. In 1853, the *Winfield Scott*, a paddlewheeled mail steamer, met its fate in the fog when it hit the rocks. Her remains are on the bottom in 30 feet of water. This location is a favorite among local divers. From this point and west to the small cove known as Bat Ray Cove is excellent shallow water diving that beginners usually find very enjoyable.

The bottom is rocky out to 40 feet where the gently sloping sand begins. The wreck is now scattered, but considering its age, a remarkable amount remains. Deepest is the spoke section of the paddlewheel, sitting flat on the bottom. It is almost unrecognizable, except for a familiar pattern of radiating spokes. The most scenic portion of the old ship is the hub of the paddlewheel in about 25 feet of water. The clear, fish-filled waters make this an excellent photo back-drop. Several large sections of the hull also remain on the bottom. Copper sheeting will catch your eye as it glimmers. Do

Garibaldi are common to Anacapa, Santa Cruz, and all the islands southward. They are not easily intimidated by divers and can actually be aggressive at times because they are very territorial. They are the most colorful fish in the Channel Islands and are protected by law.

California golden gorgonian is the most common of all the gorgonians found on the Channel Islands. In deeper water of 40 to 50 feet the strands become quite large.

not touch it, for removal of anything from this wreck is strictly prohibited. Another glimmer may be the remains of the gold that she was carrying. Stranded with her precious cargo, $885,000 in gold dust was reported salvaged. Divers occasionally have spotted tiny nuggets in the sand.

Across the Cove about 100 yards to the east is a cluster of rocks that conceal a large underwater arch. Five feet below the surface is the apex of the 20-foot arch. The surrounding waters are filled with a great deal of life and thick kelp.

Bat Ray Cove is about 1/4 to 1/2 mile to the west. A sand bottom is the dominant underwater feature. The main diving attraction has given the cove its name: a large number of big bat rays. They can be quite shy and are for the most part harmless. Approach slowly and you may be lucky enough to hand feed them as some divers have reported doing. Halibut, a consistent companion of the bat ray and a favorite quarry of local spearfishermen, can also be commonly found in these sands.

Other game in this area include some lobster, scallops and very few abalone. This is a restricted area and no invertebrates can be taken in less than 20 feet of water. Spearfishermen would do best to work on the halibut population as most other gamefish are scarce or small.

Diving on this side of the island is best done in the morning. Prevailing north or northwesterly winds can be strong in the afternoon, creating whitewater. Otherwise, the water conditions are fairly tame. Currents are generally not a problem. Visibility is not as good as other parts of the island but averages a good 30 feet anyway. Visibility at the underwater arch is somewhat less due to sand and surge.

Typical depth range	:	50 feet on inner reef, 80 on outer
Typical current conditions	:	Moderate to strong
Expertise required	:	Intermediate to advanced
Access	:	Boat

The north side of East Anacapa Island is the closest of all the Channel Islands to the mainland. However, divers pay it very little attention. Perhaps the reason is that, in this section, the taking of any aquatic life, including game, in up to 60 feet of water is prohibited. Although this area is beautiful for sightseeing and underwater photography, other parts of Anacapa can be better.

From the surface, Cathedral Cove and Cave and, at the extreme east end, Arch Rock, are breathtaking sights. There are underwater reefs below the lighthouse and 200 yards off Arch Rock. The reef under the lighthouse is marked by kelp running parallel to shore. Depths average 50 feet. The reef near the Arch Rock runs in depth about 80 feet. This reef extends west, parallel to shore at about 80 feet, to nearly the Middle Island. Visibility varies at this spot depending on the time of year. Fall is best, with water clarity that can exceed 100 feet. Early summer is the poorest because of plankton blooms. Currents are strong and frequent.

Typical depth range	:	30 to 90 feet
Typical current conditions	:	Moderate to strong, surge on shallow sections
Expertise required	:	Intermediate to advanced
Access	:	Boat

Anacapa has long been noted for excellent visibility, sea life, and although not so much in recent years, game. One of the more excellent locations around the island for all these underwater benefits is the three Parallel Reefs that lie on the backside between the West Island and the Middle Island.

The inner reef lies in 30 feet of water, the middle reef in 50 feet, and the outer reef in 70 to 90 feet. The reefs are separated by stretches of ivory sand and all reefs are covered with healthy beds of kelp.

The sea life in color and in quantity is best on the deeper reefs, although all the reefs are colorful. Gorgonians are common, including the strikingly bright red gorgonia. This beautiful invertebrate makes an excellent photo subject against the crystal clear blue waters surrounding these reefs. Other excellent photo subjects include starfish and a number of types of anemones. Tube worms and featherduster worms are also common.

Fish life surrounding the reefs include garibaldi, senoritas, opaleye, treefish and gobies. Lucky fish watchers have been known to spot an elusive giant black sea bass from time to time. Once considered a great gamefish, the black sea bass is now a protected species.

The Parallel Reefs, however, do not lack in legal gamefish. White seabass are still found over these rock outcroppings. More common gamefish include large sheepshead, yellowtail and kelp bass. Large halibut have been taken on the sand near the reefs.

Lobster reside here also, although in somewhat diminished numbers. A ''bull'' bug is still occasionally taken from here. Abalone are sparse.

Visibility is usually very good. Heavy swells can reduce water clarity on the shallower reefs, creating a strong surge. A common strong current keeps the water clear with visibility averaging 40 feet.

◄*Clear waters and a large reef area allows the diver to explore a variety of diving experiences in the Channel Islands.*

Typical depth range	:	20 to 80 feet
Typical current conditions	:	Moderate
Expertise required	:	Intermediate to advanced, novice with supervision on north side
Access	:	Boat

Because of Anacapa's small rocky land mass, water clarity is perhaps the best of all the Channel Islands. The persistent currents clean away most of the floating debris making visibility 50 feet or better. The west end of West Island gets much of this current and therefore has some of the clearest and most life-filled waters anywhere on the west coast.

The western tip of the West Island tapers off into a sharp rocky point that is an excellent habitat for some of the island's birds. On the south side, the bottom drops away at a moderate-to-quick pace, reaching as much as 80 feet within 200 yards off shore. The sloping bottom is covered with large boulders, huge cracks and crevices and a small cave or two.

On the northwest end the bottom drops away a little more gently with rocks ending in a gently sloping sand bottom at about 40 to 50 feet. This area has earned the name "Goldfish Bowl." Thick kelp forests, clear water and lots of colorful fish make this a good dive location. However, Goldfish Bowl is open to prevailing northwest winds and can become rough in the afternoon.

Supplied by the steady ocean currents, sea life is abundant and healthy on both sides. The kelp is very lush, creating a wonderland forest underwater. Purple gorgonian, usually found only in water over 90-feet deep, is common 40 feet and deeper. These delicate fans reveal their bright colors when illuminated and make excellent photo subjects. Other colorful photo subjects found here include nudibranchs, anemones, starfish and a cornucopia of colorful fish.

Anacapa has an excellent reputation for its underwater beauty, but not for its game hunting. Much of the island's reputation for being a poor game location is unjustified. At Anacapa, one simply needs to look a little harder in the right places, like west end. In many of the large cracks and small caves, it is not difficult to find several lobster—some of which can be quite large. Abalone is another quarry that can be found at this location. Pinks and reds are present but you must look hard for legal-sized abs. Those looking for scallops and game fish would do better at other parts of the island.

Hazards at this location are the current and the swells; south swells on the seaward side and rough northwest chop on the north side. The current is a persistent 1/2 to 1 knot. Watch the lie of the kelp, for 2-knot currents occasionally plague this spot, the south-facing side being the worst. Always use a current line and start your dive up current. A light swell is usually present on the south side but will show up as only a light surge in the shallow sections close to shore.

A red gorgonian leans in the nearly constant current, typical of Anacapa.

Santa Cruz Island

Santa Cruz Island is the largest of the Channel Islands, extending 21 miles in an east-west direction. It is very mountainous with several peaks reaching over 2000 feet. Like much of the Channel Islands, Santa Cruz is mostly surrounded by tall cliffs and a few sand beaches. Above the cliffs and surrounding the mountains are rolling grass-covered hills. Most of the island is used extensively for ranching. It is not unusual to see grazing cattle or sheep on the cliffs above the water.

The east end of the island is the section most frequented by divers. It is only a short jump from Anacapa and it offers the underwater game that Anacapa is often lacking. The east end is well-protected and has a multitude of dive spots to explore. Because the island is very large and variable, diving depths and conditions vary considerably at different locations.

Moving west and into slightly colder waters the sea life takes on a noticeable change. More northern varieties of invertebrates infiltrate the waters off the west end of Santa Cruz. Consequently, diving at one end of this island can be very different than at the other.

Landing on the island is by permit only. The entire island is privately owned and a permit must be obtained depending on the area visited.

A large southern portion of the island and surrounding waters fall into the Pacific Missile Test Range and, particularly in recent years, is subject to occasional closure.

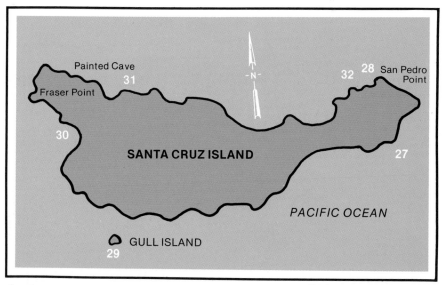

For the most popular diving, divers head for the east end of Santa Cruz. Game and terrain vary considerably throughout the island. Dive sites include: Yellowbanks (27), Scorpion Anchorage (28), Gull Island (29), Black Point and Kinton Point (30), Arch Rocks (31), and Potato Rock (32).

Typical depth range	:	30 to 80 feet
Typical current conditions	:	Moderate to strong
Expertise required	:	Intermediate to advanced
Access	:	Boat

Yellowbanks on the southeast end of Santa Cruz Island derives its name from the yellow sandstone cliffs along the shoreline. Underwater, a rocky and fairly flat reef extends from here and Middle Anchorage to the south and to over a mile out to sea. Diving depths range from 30 to 80 feet.

The flat rock bottom is occasionally broken up with small patch reefs. Although the entire bottom is abundant with life, it is at these patch reefs that divers will find the most color, particularly in the deeper (60 to 70 feet) sections. Blankets of anemones, colorful starfish and sometimes purple coral can be observed. Abalone are common, particularly red and pink abalone. In the deeper sections, bull kelp is the predominant bottom growth. This unusual kelp has one long strand that attaches to the rocks, a single air bladder that holds it 20 to 30 feet off the bottom. Long narrow blades extending from the bladder sometimes reach 30 feet in length as they billow out horizontally in the currents.

Diving Yellowbanks can be a lot of fun, but because of its open ocean location, conditions can be rough. There is a prevailing current that averages 1/2 to 2 knots. Visibility is not as good here, about 20 to 30 feet. Swells can make boat anchorage and returning to the boat tough. Diving this location is best on calm days.

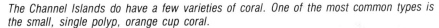

The Channel Islands do have a few varieties of coral. One of the most common types is the small, single polyp, orange cup coral.

Typical depth range	:	20 to 60 feet
Typical current conditions	:	None to light
Expertise required	:	Novice to intermediate
Access	:	Boat

Scorpion Anchorage is one of the Santa Cruz locations most frequented by divers. It is rare not to see at least one dive charter boat here on any given weekend and sometimes two or more on busy summer days. But the main reason the boatloads of divers keep coming back is not just because this spot has excellent anchorage, calm waters, or shallow depths. It is because Scorpion Anchorage has some of the best diving on Santa Cruz Island.

Scorpion Anchorage is located on the northeast end of Santa Cruz Island, only a short jump from Anacapa Island. A boat trip to Scorpion Anchorage on one of the dive charter boats from Santa Barbara, Ventura, and Channel Islands Harbors is usually less than two hours.

The Anchorage is pretty much protected from nearly all weather conditions with the exception of an occasional northeast winter storm. As a consequence, water conditions are generally very good. Visibility is usually 30 feet and often as much as 60 feet. Currents are rare and usually only on the outer edges of the reefs. Surge is almost nonexistent.

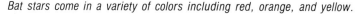

Bat stars come in a variety of colors including red, orange, and yellow.

The bright red gorgonian, wavy turban snail and red mottled fragile star are just a small sample of the abundant marine life that can be seen at Scorpion Anchorage.

The diving area is large, bordered by the large split rock to the east that separates Scorpion Anchorage from the area known as Little Scorpion and the landing cove to the west. In between are two small rocks that protrude above the water a little over 10 feet. The area around these rocks, as well as the large cracked rock, is the best for diving. The bottom is varied with many large boulders and ridges, creating an interesting habitat of overhangs, caves and crevices for animals.

The sea life is abundant and colorful. Urchins, starfish of many varieties and sea cucumbers are everywhere. Look a little closer and you will have no trouble finding colorful nudibranchs, featherduster worms and a variety of anemones. Swimming among the rocks are sheepshead, garibaldi, blue-banded gobies, and senoritas. The photographer and sightseer will no doubt find a lot to keep them busy at this dive site.

The hunter will be kept busy as well. Although this location has been dived heavily over the last several years, much game still remains. Lobster is still abundant, although big "bull" bugs are not common. Later in the season, the numbers will diminish, so hit this spot early. Abalone can also be taken in limited numbers particularly in shallow water where many divers fail to look. Look deeper for some unusually big scallops. As for the game fish, look for the large kelp bass that lurk in the sparse kelp. Halibut can sometimes be found over the sand on the seaward side of the reefs.

Although the bottom topography is irregular, it slopes gently to about 40 to 60 feet and ends in sand. This deeper area where the rocks meet the sand is excellent for photos of the brightly colored red gorgonian. The shallow areas 50 to 100 yards off the beach are excellent for beginners and students. The conditions are great and there is much to see.

Near Scorpion Anchorage, on a 66-foot-deep sand bottom, is the wreck of the *Peacock*. This wreck is described by many divers as one of the most picturesque in all the Channel Islands. She is a 140-foot-long wooden minesweeper with most of the hull intact. The wreck tops out at only 40 feet below the surface, making this a fairly easy dive.

Typical depth range	:	30 to 80 feet, deeper on seaward side
Typical current conditions	:	Moderate, surge on shallow reefs
Expertise required	:	Intermediate to advanced
Access	:	Boat

Gull Island, on the seaward side of Santa Cruz Island, has been described by many as one of the most picturesque dive spots in all of the northern Channel Islands. From the surface, Gull Island is little more than a large rock surrounded by many smaller rocks. This creates a treacherous sea for all boats. These rocks indicate an extensive system of spectacular reefs and kelp beds.

Gull Island lies on the southern side of Santa Cruz Island, a little more than a thousand yards out. Protected from west-northwest wind that is predominate in this area, Gull Island offers more calm and clear waters. A southern swell can, however, make the spot a difficult dive. There are occasionally strong currents, but these can be carefully avoided by diving in just the right spot, sometimes behind some of the rocks.

Reefs surround the small island and extend as much as 100 yards seaward and toward Santa Cruz Island. Many of the reefs are within only a few feet of the surface. Much of submerged rocky areas drop vertically in small walls. In other locations, the reefs spread out from the main rocks in fingers surrounded by sand. Ledges, overhangs, and small caves are common. The sea bottom at Gull Island varies, with corners for everyone to explore and enjoy.

The photographer and sightseer will fare best. Visibility is excellent with the average 40 feet. Sea life on the bottom is equally spectacular. Red gorgonian, colorful anemones, and flashy nudibranchs are common. More rare, beautiful California or purple hydrocoral can be found under ledges in deeper water. A variety of starfish and featherduster worms will also delight the photographer's eye. Away from the rocks, fish are everywhere. Seals are also frequent visitors. All of this is covered by a canopy of giant kelp.

Hunters will certainly enjoy the scenery, but they will not do as well here as in other less-worked parts of Santa Cruz Island. Because Gull Island is a popular dive spot, game is worked over; however, the small rocky island has so many reefs, crevices, and rocks that it is uncommon for a diver to come away empty handed. Lobster, scallops and especially abalone, are still present in sufficient quantities. Spearfishing is also good. Kelp bass and sheepshead are the most common. Halibut rest in the sand surrounding some of the reefs. On the outer reef fringes, over deeper water, pelagic fish sometimes pass by.

Morse Point juts out from shore to the west in a series of shallow rocky reefs. Diving is similar to Gull Island with steep drops and many rocks to explore. There is a lush kelp forest and visibility is excellent. ➤

Typical depth range	:	30 to 60 feet
Typical current conditions	:	Moderate to strong, some surge
Expertise required	:	Intermediate to advanced
Access	:	Boat

The most remote section of Santa Cruz Island is the stretch of shoreline on the southwest end between Fraser Point and Morse Point. Within this stretch of shore are the rocky points known as Black Point and Kinton Point. Both are excellent hunting grounds for abalone and gamefish.

The bottom configuration is similar in both locations. Rocky reefs, some of which run parallel to shore, extend out from the points into water 30 to 60 feet deep. Most of the reefs are covered with tall stalks of kelp that are frequently bent over from the strength of the current. On these reefs it is not difficult to acquire the limit of abalone in one dive. Red, pinks and even an occasional rare white or Sorenson abalone, the most tender of the abalone family, can be found here.

For the spearfisherman, big halibut is the name of the game. The rocky reefs and the points themselves are separated by large sand bottoms that the halibut love. Rockfish, sheepshead and other fish are available as well. Lobster, however, can be hard to find. Looking in the shallow water may help but surge can be a problem.

Visibility runs only 20 to 30 feet, making other parts of the island better for clear water. The photographer and sightseer will enjoy the world of the numerous invertebrates. Nudibranchs, bright red anemones and a variety of sponges make this dive an enjoyable experience.

Currents can run strong. Look at the lay of the kelp which will indicate the current strength and direction. Remember to always dive up current. The area is somewhat protected from the prevailing weather but large swells occasionally hit the area.

Tube anemones live in patches of sand and silt near reefs. Their long arms dangle in the current waiting for a bit of food to pass. They come in a range of colors including orange, and occasionally purple.

Typical depth range	:	20 to 40 feet
Typical current conditions	:	Light to moderate, some surge
Expertise required	:	Intermediate to advanced, novice with supervision
Access	:	Boat

Much of the front side on the west end of Santa Cruz Island is volcanic cliffs that are honeycombed with caves and rocky coves. There are numerous coves, large and small, in this area. Some of the more noteworthy dive points in this area include Arch Rocks, Diablo Point, and Platts Harbor.

At most of these dive spots the bottom drops away from the cliffs moderately in a jumble of rocks that have broken from the cliffs above. The rocks end in clean ivory-colored sand at about 40 feet. In some locations small reefs and large boulders lie slightly offshore. Kelp is sparse and patchy.

Tasty rock scallops are abundant along this entire section of the island. They can be tricky to spot (look for the red "smile" before they close) but are well worth the effort it takes to pry them from the rocks. Try them raw right from the shell—Great! Other game include a few lobster and halibut that are found over the sand.

A steady, passive current keeps the water clean and clear. Averaging 35 feet, the visibility is seldom poor. Surge and heavy seas can be avoided by diving this location in the morning before the usual north to northwest afternoon winds come up.

The clear, usually calm and fairly shallow waters make for pleasant and casual sightseeing. Look for colorful starfish. There are caves that go deep into the cliffs. Explore them at your own risk and with proper training and equipment. There is, however, little of interest on the insides of most of these caves.

The number of species and variations of colors in which anemones come will keep the macro-photographer very busy.

Typical depth range	:	20 to 80 feet
Typical current conditions	:	Moderate, some surge
Expertise required	:	Intermediate to advanced
Access	:	Boat

Located on the northwest side of the east end, Potato Rock is a pyramid-shaped rock that sits on the western edge of the mouth of a deep cove known as Potato Harbor. About 200 yards offshore from this rock, a pinnacle rises from a bottom depth of 90 feet to within 10 feet of the surface. The resulting walls and ledges of the pinnacle provide a habitat for a huge variety of marine life that will delight the photographer, sightseer and hunter.

The most spectacular section of the pinnacle is the vertical wall on the northeast side. Dropping from 10 to 80 feet straight down, the wall is home for a multitude of colorful anemones, featherworms, and nudibranchs.

The sheer face of the underwater pinnacle at Potato Rock holds a number of anemones.

Painted Cave

On the northwest end of Santa Cruz Island are spectacular cliffs of volcanic rock that are permeated by a number of large caves. The largest of these caves is the Painted Cave. Painted Cave is large enough that, with the proper sea conditions, some daring and experienced dive charter boat captains can and will pull the entire boat far into the cave. This is a thrilling experience.

The cave goes into the side of the island over 500 feet. Much of the full length of the cave can be explored by a small inflatable boat or dinghy. Inside, the walls of the cave are spotted with patches of blue and orange oxides. They appear to have been painted; hence the name "Painted Cave."

Exploring the cave requires calm seas. Anchorage is poor outside the entrance. If you use a dinghy, leave someone behind on the main boat. There are many other caves in the vicinity that can easily be confused with Painted Cave. Diving conditions in and around the cave are poor. There is much better underwater exploring to the east and around the point to the west.

Coupled with the traditional good visibility of Channel Island, this is an underwater photographer's paradise. The range and quantity of colorful hues is breathtaking. Photographers using a macro lens will be especially satisfied.

On the southwest side of the pinnacle, it drops off steeply in a series of ledges. Here, you will also find a large quantity of anemones, feather-worms, nudibranchs and starfish.

For the hunter, rock scallops abound in sufficient quantities all over the rocks and many are fairly large. Much of this side of the island seems to be blessed with a good quantity of large rock scallops. Some gamefish can be found on the southwest side. For lobster and abalone try closer to shore.

The pinnacle can come dangerously close to the surface during low tide or moderate swells. There is no kelp on the rock to help mark its location. If you plan to take your own boat, obtain good charts, use a depth finder and use caution in anchoring. As always, navigating the Channel Islands is best left to the experienced skipper.

Surge and currents in this area can be tricky, but close observation and a little help from an experienced divemaster should prove helpful.

Santa Rosa Island

West of Santa Cruz Island and east of San Miguel is the second largest of the Channel Islands, Santa Rosa Island. It is 15 miles long and 10 miles wide. This is an island of contrasts, for along with its sharp shoreline cliffs, there are also long sandy beaches and even a coastal marsh on the east end, an unusual feature for the Channel Islands. Its surface is dominated by high mountains and deep canyons that give way to rolling hills and terraces. The surface of this island is perhaps the most alive of all the northern chain. Freshwater (not good for drinking) springs and streams that dump into the marsh support frogs, fox, skunk and other animals on the rolling hills.

Second only to San Nicolas Island, game is the main reason most divers come to this island. The island is so untouched that a great deal of abalone, lobster and halibut can still be found. Most of the island is surrounded by large kelp beds that further support the growth of underwater game.

Sightseers and photographers will enjoy Santa Rosa. On the ocean bottom is sea life in forms and colors not always seen on the more southern islands. Water clarity, however, is not as good as the other island waters. Averaging about 30 feet, it still provides for an enjoyable dive. Selecting the right spots will net visibility sometimes over 50 feet.

Unfortunately, the further north and west you go in the Channel Islands chain, the more intense the weather can become. Santa Rosa can take a beating from time to time, but calm water can be found in plenty of coves around the island.

Landing is prohibited without permit because the island is privately owned by Vail & Vickers, a cattle ranching company.

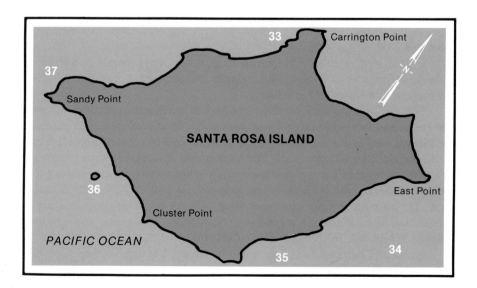

Typical depth range	:	20 to 80 feet
Typical current conditions	:	Moderate, some surge
Expertise required	:	Intermediate to advanced, novice with supervision on calm, shallow sections of Beacon Reef
Access	:	Boat

The northernmost point of Santa Rosa Island is Carrington Point. The point is a rocky 400 feet high. A quarter mile off the point to the north is the popular Beacon Reef.

Beacon Reef tops out at only 12 feet and drops moderately to 80 feet. This reef is popular because it serves a variety of diving skills and needs. The beginning divers can concentrate on the shallower rocks while more experienced divers may wish to pursue game and take photos deeper.

There is much for the sightseer to explore, but the visibility here is not as good as other parts of the island. The visibility averages only about 20 feet because of a current running through the channel. Watch the lay of the kelp near the shallow section of the reef and adjust your dive accordingly.

To the west are a series of rarely dove underwater pinnacles that can be excellent for hunting and exploring. They are as shallow as 45 feet, but most average 60 feet at the top and up to 90 feet at the bottom. Still further to the west and slightly closer to shore is the wave-battered Rodes Reef. This is another location not often dove, mainly because it is open to the prevailing northwest weather. When calm, this can be a good dive in depths over 40 feet. In shallow water, the surge is strong, and the terrain is mainly barren. This entire north coast water is fairly shallow, with diving depths of 70 feet or less extending almost two miles off shore. Much of the bottom is flat rock with an occasional pinnacle or reef. An experienced skipper should be able to place divers on interesting deep reefs that are seldom explored by divers. Rough seas, bottom surge and only mediocre visibility make this north side section of the island a spot for the experienced diver. Beginners should stick to Beacon Reef.

◀Santa Rosa Island is surrounded by plush kelp forests that harbor many varieties of marine life. Beacon Reef and North Shoreline (33), East End Pinnacles (34), Bee Rock and the Western Shoreline (36), and Talcott Shoals (37) are among the recommended dive sites.

Typical depth range	:	40 to 70 feet on the inner pin-nacles, 50 to 100 feet on the outer pinnacles
Typical current conditions	:	Moderate to strong
Expertise required	:	Intermediate to advanced
Access	:	Boat

At the extreme eastern end of the Santa Rosa Island is East Point. At 700 yards, and then again at 4000 yards, almost due south of the point, the sea bottom rises to a scattered group of pinnacles that are from 10 to 30 feet high and within 40 feet of the surface. These reefs can be divided into two groups. The first group, nearer to the shore, supports a huge kelp bed and large variety of marine animals. The second group, much farther off shore, has little or no giant kelp, but is excellent for game.

The group nearer to shore is easily identified by the large kelp bed. The depths range from 40 to 70 feet. The rocks and reefs lie in a wide variety of channels, ledges and drop-offs. The varying bottom provides an excellent environment for lobster, abalone and scallops. Most game fish can be found here including kelp bass, sheepshead and, on the sand near the reefs, halibut.

Much of the same conditions exist on the outer pinnacles. The outer pinnacles rise 85 to 100 feet and are within 40 to 50 feet of the surface. These pinnacles lack the tall kelp cover of the inner reef, but they are still enriched with a huge variety and volume of marine life. Large gamefish and shellfish can also be seen here.

Both areas are superb for the photographer and sightseer. The marine life found on the rocks is colorful and varied. The types of starfish found here include leather star, giant-spined star, and the beautiful purplish sun-flower star. The huge sunflower star can reach 90 cm. in diameter. There is a large number of anemones on these reefs, and these colorful creatures make excellent photo subjects. Other striking subjects, attached to the rocks, include nudibranchs and feather worms.

Water conditions around the pinnacles are generally very good. The visibility averages over 40 feet; however, plankton blooms can reduce visibility somewhat in the late spring through early summer. The area is pro-tected from the prevailing west-northwest weather and is relatively calm, even far offshore. Currents, however, can be strong, particularly on the outer pinnacles.

Typical depth range	:	20 to 70 feet
Typical current conditions	:	Light to moderate
Expertise required	:	Intermediate to advanced, novice with supervision
Access	:	Boat

Boats seeking refuge from the often strong northwesterly winds will often head for Johnson's Lee and Ford Point on the backside of Santa Rosa Island. The coves here provide good anchorage and excellent diving in calm waters.

Johnson's Lee is just to the east of South Point, the southernmost point of the island. On shore is an abandoned military base and a rotting pier. To the north of the pier is a reef covered by a lush kelp forest and surrounded by a great deal of sea life.

Ford Point and the small cove to the east have good anchorage. There is good diving near the point and next to the cliffs.

At both locations, underwater photographers and sightseers will enjoy the plentiful marine life and clear waters. Visibility is the best Santa Rosa Island has to offer, averaging over 30 feet. Diving depths at both spots are fairly reasonable, with no steep drops and average reef depth of 40 feet.

Hunting at these spots will produce abalone, lobster and gamefish such as rockfish and halibut.

Nudibranchs are a favorite of photographers that visit the Channel Islands.

Typical depth range	:	40 to 80 feet
Typical current conditions	:	Moderate, often strong surge
Expertise required	:	Intermediate to advanced
Access	:	Boat

The back side of Santa Rosa Island, between Sandy Point and what is known as China Camp, is a series of sand beaches broken up by rocky points and reefs that extend seaward. Along the entire shore is a shallow bottom covered with rocky reefs and kelp patches. This is the most remote section of the island and consequently has a lot of good hunting grounds.

Large red and pink abalone are abundant. Gamefish hunting is also good. Rockfish, sheepshead, big halibut, lobster, and sometimes white sea bass can be found.

The most noteworthy dive locations are Cluster Point to the south, Bee Rock, out to sea a mile or so, and the south side of Sandy Point.

Bee Rock drops steeply on all sides 60 to 80 feet. The water surrounding the rock is clear and filled with schools of fish. The rocky reefs are covered with an array of colorful invertebrates. If the weather is good this is an excellent spot to visit.

Cluster Point is small, surrounded by many small rocks that just break the surface and create a swirl of whitewater over 200 yards from shore. Reefs extend out from these rocks that are interesting to explore, but are barren in comparison to Bee Rock.

The water conditions are the main drawback of this spot. The entire section is open to frequent large swells and surge on the bottom can be a problem on the shallower reefs. The best time to dive this area is in the fall.

The blackeye goby is about three to four inches long and lives on rocks and near reef edges.

Typical depth range	:	20 to 100 feet
Typical current conditions	:	Moderate, strong surge
Expertise required	:	Intermediate to advanced
Access	:	Boat

Off the northwest end of Santa Rosa is a 20-square-mile area of shallow water known as Talcott Shoals. Diving depths range from 100 feet to as shallow as 10 feet, causing the sea to boil and break. The shallower sections are a series of ledges and the deeper bottom is flat rock broken up by ledges and reefs.

Because of the size of the shoals, the type and quality of diving is variable. Toward shore, visibility drops to as little as 10 feet. Some of the shallow sections, 20 feet or less, are fairly boring and barren, and there is some surge. If you drop into the right spots there is much to see. On the outer sections, visibility can reach 50 feet, but beware of possible currents. Unfortunately, surge on the bottom is a common problem.

There are two wrecks on the shoals: the *Golden Horn* and the *Aggi*. The *Golden Horn* is a wreck from 1892 and lies in 15 feet of water. It is a good spot for lobster. The shallow water makes this a spot diveable only on calm days since surge can be a problem. The *Aggi*, a 265-foot-long steel wreck, is in 60 to 80 feet of water. This is a good spot for large fish and abalone.

Much of the shoals is covered by kelp, but in some areas the kelp is sparse. Holes and ledges usually hold lobster and abalone. Gamefish are also plentiful, especially large sheepshead and the elusive white sea bass, prize game of hard-core California spearfishermen.

The winds here prevail from the north by northwest. Consequently, Talcott Shoals can be very open to rough seas. It takes an experienced skipper to choose just when and where to dive on the shoals.

It pays to look closely for colorful sea life at Talcott Shoals.

San Miguel Island

San Miguel Island receives the full brunt of the weather coming off the Pacific Ocean. It is the last and westernmost in the Channel Islands chain. Because of its remoteness and constant battering by the seas, it is an awesome island of barren beauty. San Miguel is about eight miles long and four miles wide. For the most part it is a plateau where the only surface features are two hills that rise above the flat top.

The island is rich in history. Juan Rodriquez Cabrillo, discoverer of the Channel Islands, died and is reported buried here, although his grave has never been located. The Navy at one time used the island as a gunnery range and then as a missile range. It still falls in the Navy's jurisdiction, but it is under administration of the National Park Service.

Landing on the island is now possible through permits issued by the National Park Service. Upon landing, it is required that you have a park ranger with you at all times. No camping is allowed on the island. There are several miles of hiking trails on the island for use during daytime only. Some of the most spectacular vistas on the islands can be seen from these trails.

The bottom of the sea is as rugged as the island terrain. Drop-offs, ledges and large reefs with huge kelp beds are all available to dive. Visibility is generally excellent, and there is a lot of game (except lobster—they prefer warmer waters). There are spots that the beginners can enjoy, but divers should generally have some experience when diving San Miguel's waters.

Because of its remoteness, openness to weather conditions, and hidden dangers in the water, only the most experienced skippers should travel to this island. Professional dive charter boat captains are well aware of the hazards and limitations that this harsh island offers. They are the best guides to diving its spectacular reefs. If you plan a trip to this island, don't get dead-set on diving it, for approaching the island is often a "weather-permitting" situation.

The eight-mile-long San Miguel Island usually falls prey to rough weather and the constant battering of the ocean that has created a high plateau. The most interesting dive sites include: Wyckoff Ledge and Tyler Bight (38), Cuyler Harbor (39), and Wilson's Rock (40). ➤

Drop-offs, ledges, and large reefs with huge kelp beds around San Miguel Island harbor many varieties of starfish.

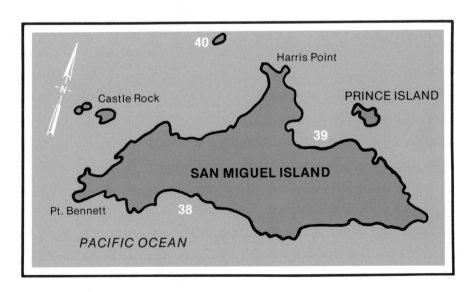

Typical depth range	:	Averages 40 feet at Tyler; sharp drops to 120 feet at Wyckoff Ledge
Typical current conditions	:	Moderate, surge
Expertise required	:	Intermediate or advanced, depending on conditions
Access	:	Boat

The area most protected from the weather on San Miguel Island offers some of the island's most exciting diving. The prevailing winds whip in from the north-northwest at speeds that sometimes exceed 40 knots. Protected from those winds, the south side of the island enjoys calm waters over much of the year. Out from shore, west of Crook Point, are several spectacular reefs and underwater pinnacles. Tyler Bight is a sandy cove full of these reefs. East of Tyler Bight is the famous Wyckoff Ledge.

Wyckoff Ledge rises from a sand bottom 120 feet down. The top lies in 10 feet of water. There is a single sheer drop from 20 feet to 90 feet. This is California wall-diving at its best. The wall is covered with colorful anemones, scallops, tube worms, and other invertebrates. On the top of the rock is a series of small ledges. Game hunting is limited to scallops and a large quantity of ocean-going fish.

The giant-spined starfish and an array of invertebrates, can be found at Wyckoff Ledge.

The "bloom" of the rose anemone adorns the rocky reefs at Tyler Bight.

Inside Tyler Bight are a number of rocky reefs covered with kelp. Some of the rocks lie quite shallow, and caution must be used in the maneuvering and anchoring of vessels. The drop-offs on these reefs are somewhat more tame. Small, rocky ledges and walls are common, and most drop only a few feet. The average depth inside the Bight is around 40 feet. Abalone and lobster can be found but are for the most part scarce. The underwater scenery is the main event here.

Visibility, particularly along the Wyckoff Ledge, is excellent. The water is deep, blue, and clear because of a generally mild current. This is considered the lee (calm) side of the island, but winter storms and swells coming from the south are not unusual. Be prepared for bottom surge in the shallows.

Typical depth range	:	30 to 60 feet
Typical current conditions	:	Weak
Expertise required	:	Intermediate, novice with super-vision
Access	:	Boat

Perhaps the most beautiful place to anchor at San Miguel Island is in Cuyler Harbor. It is thrilling to sit in the peaceful waters and imagine how Juan Rodriquez Cabrillo, the discoverer of the Channel Islands, spent his last days here more than four and a half centuries ago. It is here that this courageous explorer died, and it is believed that he is buried on this island or nearby Prince Island with his jewel-encrusted sword. The grave has never been found—but there is a monument to this great man on the island, overlooking the harbor.

The shoreline of the crescent-shaped bay is a long stretch of clean white sand. On the sea bottom is a conglomeration of reefs that could take weeks to explore completely. Clover, Cans, and Middle Rocks are a few of the reef names.

Anchorage in the harbor is actually difficult and hazardous. A number of the reefs break the surface or lie just below the waterline. Skippers must use caution to insure that the anchor does not slip, allowing their vessel to drift into the hidden rocks.

Healthy kelp beds fill most of the harbor. The sand bottom from which the rocky reefs lie averages 50 feet in depth. The reefs vary in height from a few feet to large rock faces that ascend almost vertically over 30 feet. There are lots of crevices and overhangs to explore.

Inside the thick kelp and around the rocks, abalone and fish are plentiful. Photographers will enjoy the variety of unusual types of invertebrates attached to the reefs. Large purplish sunflower stars and the brightly colored rose anemone can be found. Both make excellent photo subjects. The clear water and sunlight filtering through the thick kelp create an excellent backdrop for all types of photographs.

The harbor is protected from the heavy weather that is common to San Miguel Island. Heavy swells can hit the harbor if the weather is coming from the north; therefore, anchorage is best sought elsewhere. Currents are infrequent and usually weak. Observe the lay of the kelp for any indications of current. Visibility is quite good, averaging 40 to 50 feet.

Working the rocks toward Harris Point will produce excellent diving. Nifty Rock and Hare Rock are just a couple of the rocks marking reefs along the shore toward the point. The reefs offer good diving in clear water with much to see and a lot of abalone.

Typical depth range	:	Vertical drops to 150 feet, ledges at 35 and 60 feet
Typical current conditions	:	Moderate to strong, surge
Expertise required	:	Advanced, intermediate with supervision when calm
Access	:	Boat

Diving San Miguel Island, the westernmost of the Channel Islands chain, can be one of the most enjoyable dives in California. Diving Wilson's Rock, about two miles off the island's northwestern end, can be simply delightful.

The quantity, diversity and color of sea life surrounding the remote Wilson's Rock is almost staggering. At times the life on the rock face is so thick, it seems to be layered. Circulating the rock is deep blue, crystal clear, life-filled waters that are frequented by several ocean-going varieties of fish.

Wilson's Rock is indeed a good location for the spearfisherman. Very large rockfish, including the colorful vermillion rockfish, are seen here. Scallops can be found on the deeper sections, and most are the size of saucers. The sheer rock faces and lack of kelp, however, cause abalone and lobster hunting to be poor.

Sections of the wall drop straight down to as much as 180 feet. Coupled with usually superb visibility, Wilson's Rock is one of the most breathtaking dive spots in all of the Channel Islands. Ledges are present at several depths. The most prominant are at 35, and at 60 to 70 feet.

Diving the rock can present difficulties. Approach is possible only on rare calm days. Open to almost all weather conditions, the rock can only be dived a few days out of the year. Anchoring on or near the rock is extremely difficult, and it should only be attempted by the most experienced skippers. The rock is adjacent to dangerous reefs on the west and in one spot to the south.

Surge can be severe in the shallower sections, but it can be easily avoided by moving to the deeper, more attractive diving areas. The rock wall drops off vertically to more than 150 feet in depth. Watch your depths and bottom times carefully. Currents are also common. Listen to your divemasters and follow their directions carefully. With a little extra caution and planning, diving Wilson's Rock can be an extremely rewarding experience.

The furthest extension of the Channel Islands is Richardson's Rock, which is much farther out to sea beyond Wilson's Rock. Divers rarely dive this spot because of rough weather and its remote location. Conditions are similar to those at Wilson's Rock, with vertical drop-offs to deep water, excellent visibility, lots of gamefish and big scallops. Purple coral has been seen here as well. Diving here is a challenge for the experienced diver, but it can be a thrill for those lucky to catch it on a calm day.

3

Safety

Diving the Channel Islands should be a very safe and enjoyable experience. Although conditions here are certainly a little more harsh than at some tropical islands, there is no reason why diving cannot be as safe or safer if certain factors are considered.

Cold Water. With water temperatures in the 60s Fahrenheit, hypothermia (a lowering of the body temperature due to external cold) can be a problem. Always dive with a good-fitting wetsuit or drysuit, and a hood. Hypothermia can be dangerous because it accelerates respiration, deteriorates muscular coordination, and can even cloud thinking. A chilled body is also at higher risk of decompression sickness. Always allow for an extra margin of error in the dive tables when severely chilled.

Deep Diving. Depths should *not* be a problem when diving the Channel Islands. The most interesting dive sites are shallower than 80 feet. With few exceptions, there is little else to see deeper than 80 feet. The exceptions include a few wrecks and offshore pinnacles. Do not go deeper than 90 feet unless you have a specific goal and have planned your dive carefully. Try to keep most of your diving depths 70 feet or shallower. Again, this is where there is the most to see in the Channel Islands. Always watch your times, depths, and tank pressure carefully on all dives, including shallow ones. Because most of your dives will be in relatively shallow water it is possible to make several dives a day. It is important to carefully consult your repetitive dive tables. Know how to use them and always calculate your bottom time *before* your next dive.

Currents. Currents are another possible hazard of diving the Channel Islands. Current strength and direction depends much on location and time of the dive. Most dive charter boat operators do *not* make drift dives. Watch the lay of the kelp as this will indicate current strength and direction. Also watch for swirling waters off the stern of the boat. Always dive up-current and use a current line. A current line is a long (100 yards or more) floating line, usually with a float at one end, that trails behind the boat in the current. Should the diver surface behind the boat, the diver grabs the line and pulls himself hand-over-hand back to the boat. Diving in currents is covered in chapter 2, "Diving the Channel Islands."

Hazardous Marine Life. Information on hazardous marine life and on diving in kelp is included in chapter 2, "Diving the Channel Islands."

Safety Recommendations. To make your dives in the Channel Islands as safe and as enjoyable as possible, four things are recommended. First, consult a divemaster familiar with waters you wish to dive. Almost all dive charter boats have a divemaster on board. He or she can inform you as to specifics on currents, bottom topography, marine life, and other details important to your dive.

Second, plan your dive and dive your plan. Discuss with your buddy cut-off depth (the deepest you wish to go), bottom times, direction of travel, and purpose of dive (sightseeing, hunting, photos, etc.).

Third, be in good physical condition. There is no need to be ready for a marathon, but you should be able to run around the block a couple of times with no problem. Much of the diving on the Channel Islands is easy, while other dive spots are challenging. Be sure that you are in good enough physical condition to handle the type of diving desired and any emergency that may arise.

And finally, KNOW YOUR LIMITATIONS. Diving into something that you cannot physically or mentally handle will not only make the dive unenjoyable, but it could be very dangerous. Know when to sit the dive out.

Diving Accidents. Should a diving accident occur, it is important to first stabilize the victim and then get him to the proper facilities as soon as possible.

If you are on shore, call 911. This is the emergency phone number now in effect throughout California. Emergency aid will be dispatched quickly. You may also call (213) 590-2225, which is the number of the U.S. Coast Guard Emergency Coordination Center.

If you are on a boat, call for assistance from the U.S. Coast Guard on channel 16 on a VHF marine band radio. Should they determine the accident to be serious in nature, they will medi-vac the victim to the proper facilities. The decompression chambers presently used by the Coast Guard are located at Los Robles Hospital in Thousand Oaks, the chamber facility at the Isthmus on Catalina Island operated by USC Medical Center, and the chamber facility in San Diego operated by the UCSD. Remember, always be sure to tell them if the accident is diving-related so they can have the proper facilities readied.

Appendix

Dive Operations

LOS ANGELES COUNTY: SOUTH BAY AND MALIBU

Scuba Haus, 2501 Wilshire Blvd., Santa Monica, CA; (213) 828-2916
Malibu Divers Inc., 21231 Pacific Coast Hwy., Malibu, CA; (213) 456-2396
The Dive Shop, 8642 Wilshire Blvd., Beverly Hills, CA; (213) 652-4990
New England Divers, 11830 W. Pico Blvd., West Los Angeles, CA; (213) 477-5021
Marina Del Rey Divers, 2539 Lincoln Blvd., Marine Del Rey, CA; (213) 827-1131
Dive 'N Surf, 504 W. Broadway, Redondo Beach, CA; (213) 372-8423
Sea D' Sea, 1911 Catalina Ave, Redondo Beach, CA; (213) 373-6355
American Institute of Diving, 1901 Pacific Coast Hwy., Lomita, CA; (213) 326-6663
Catalina Divers Supply, Pleasure Pier, Avalon Catalina Island, CA; (213) 510-0330

LOS ANGELES COUNTY: SAN FERNANDO VALLEY

Scuba Duba Dive, 7126 Reseda Blvd., Reseda, CA; (818) 881-4545
West Coast Divers Supply, 16931 Sherman Way, Van Nuys, CA; (818) 708-8136/8137
Aloha Diving Schools, 7626 Tampa Ave., Reseda, CA; (818) 343-6343
Aloha Diving Schools, 2910 W. Magnolia, Burbank, CA; (818) 846-1320
Laguna Sea Sports, 6959 Van Nuys Blvd., Van Nuys, CA; (818) 787-7066
Sport Chalet Divers, 920 Foothill Blvd., La Canada, CA; (818) 790-2717
Cal Aquatics, 22725 Ventura Blvd., Woodland Hills, CA; (818) 346-4799

LOS ANGELES COUNTY: SOUTHEAST AREA

Divers Corner, 11200 Old River School Rd., Downey, CA; (213) 927-1417
New England Divers, 4148 Viking Way, Long Beach, CA; (213) 421-8939, (714) 827-5110
Scuba Schools of Long Beach, 4740 Pacific Coast Hwy., Long Beach, CA; (213) 494-4740

LOS ANGELES COUNTY: NORTHEAST AREA

Sport Diving West, Inc., 11501 Whittier Blvd., Whittier, CA; (213) 692-7373
Divers West, 2695 Foothill Blvd., #A, Pasadena, CA; (818) 796-4287
Gucciones Scuba Habitat, 3220-B S. Brea Canyon Rd., Diamond Bar, CA; (714) 594-7927
Southern California Diving Center, 1121 S. Glendora Ave., W. Covina, CA; (818) 338-8863

SAN BERNARDINO COUNTY

Sea-To-Sea Scuba School, 10950 S. Mt. Vernon Ave., Colton, CA: (714) 825-2502
Undersea Showcase, 1335 W. Foothill Blvd., Upland, CA; (714) 946-2266

RIVERSIDE COUNTY

Laguna Sea Sports, 6343 Magnolia Blvd., Riverside, CA; (714) 683-6244

SANTA BARBARA COUNTY

The Dive Shop of Santa Maria, 1975 B. South Broadway, Santa Maria, CA; (805) 922-0076
Dive West Sports, 115 W. Main, Santa Maria, CA; (805) 925-5878
Watersports Unltd., 732 North H St., Lompoc, CA; (805) 736-1800
Bob's Diving Locker, 500 Botello Road, Goleta, CA; (805) 967-4456
Divers Supply of Santa Barbara, 5854 Hollister Ave., Goleta, CA; (805) 964-0180
Aquatics of Santa Barbara, 5370 Hollister #3, Santa Barbara, CA; (805) 964-8689
Divers Den, 22 Anacapa St., Santa Barbara, CA; (805) 963-8917
Underwater Sports, Breakwater Harbor, Santa Barbara, CA; (805) 962-5400

VENTURA COUNTY

Far West Marine Center, Thousand Oaks, Simi Valley, Canyon Country, CA;
(805) 495-3600, (805) 522-2628, (805) 252-6955
Aquatics, 295 Channel Islands Blvd., Port Hueneme, CA; (805) 984-DIVE
Ocean Antics, 2359 E. Thompson, Ventura, CA; (805) 652-1600
American Institute of Diving, 1901 Pacific Coast Hwy., Lomita, CA; (213) 326-6663
Catalina Divers Supply, Pleasure Pier, Avalon, Catalina Island, CA; (213) 510-0330
Poncho's Dive & Tackle, 3600 Cabazone Way, Oxnard, CA; (805) 985-4788
Ventura Scuba School, 1559 Spinnaker #108, Ventura, CA; (805) 656-0167
Aqua Ventures, 1001 S. Harbor Blvd., Oxnard, CA; (805) 985-8861

ORANGE COUNTY: NORTHERN AREA

Openwater Habitat Marine School, 411 South Main St., Orange, CA; 1-800-334,6467,
(714) 633-7283
Diver's Mart, 2036 W. Whittier, La Habra, CA; (213) 694-1311
Scuba Toys, 9547 Valley View, Cypress, CA; (714) 527-0430
Scuba Toys, Too, 1640 W. Lincoln, Anaheim, CA; (714) 956-5540
Sea Ventures, 350 E. Orangethorpe #2, Placentia, CA; (714) 993-3211
Scuba World, 1706 Tustin, Orange, CA; (714) 998-6382
Ocean Sports Ltd., 3141 Yorba Linda Blvd., Fullerton, CA; (714) 996-1970

ORANGE COUNTY: SOUTHERN AREA

Black Barts Aquatics, 34145 Coast Hwy., Dana Point, CA; (714) 496-5891
Black Barts Aquatics, 24882 Muirlands, El Toro, CA; (714) 855-2323
Aquatic Center, 4535 Coast Hwy., Newport Beach, CA; (714) 650-5440
Adventures in Diving, 31678 Coast Hwy., South Laguna, CA; (714) 499-4517
Mr. Scuba, 1031 S. Coast Hwy., Laguna Beach, CA; (714) 494-4146
The Dive Shop, 16475 Harbor Blvd., Fountain Valley, CA; (714) 531-5838
National Scuba, 16442 A Gothard St., Huntington Beach, CA; (714) 847-4386
Sport Chalet Divers. 16242 Beach Blvd., Huntington Beach, CA; (714) 848-0988
Laguna Sea Sports, 2146 Newport Blvd., Costa Mesa, CA; (714) 645-5820
Laguna Sea Sports, 925 N. Coast Hwy., Laguna Beach, CA; (714) 494-6965
Ocean Sports Ltd., 5046 Edinger Ave., Huntington Beach, CA; (213) 592-2506,
(714) 840-4840

SAN DIEGO COUNTY: NORTHERN AREA

Diving Locker Aquatics, 348 East Grand, Escondido, CA; (619) 746-8980
Ocean Enterprises, 267 El Camino Real, Encinitas, CA; (619) 942-3661
Diving Locker Aquatics, 405 N. Highway 101, Solana Beach, CA; (619) 755-6822
Sport Chalet Divers, Vineyard Shopping Center, Escondido, CA; (619) 746-5958

SAN DIEGO COUNTY: SOUTHERN AREA

Water Education Training (W.E.T.), 7094 Miramar Rd., San Diego, CA;
(619) 578-DIVE (3483)

San Diego Divers Supply, 7522 La Jolla Blvd., La Jolla, CA; (619) 459-2691

Diving Locker Aquatics, 1020 Grand Ave., San Diego, CA; (619) 272-1120

New England Divers, 3860 Rosecrans St., San Diego, CA; (619) 298-0531

Ocean Enterprises, 4646 Convoy St., San Diego, CA; (619) 565-6054

San Diego Divers Supply, 4004 Sports Arena Blvd., San Diego, CA; (619) 224-3439

National City Divers Supply, 105 W. 18th, National City, CA; (619) 477-5946

Ocean Stuff Dive Shop, 2434 South Port Way #E, National City, CA; (619) 477-5946

Ward's Dry Dock, 2198 Hwy. 86, El Centro, CA; (619) 352-2033

Sports Chalet Divers, 5500 Grossmont Ctr. Dr., La Mesa, CA; (619) 463-9381

Dive Charter Boats

INDIVIDUALIZED DIVE TRIPS FOR SMALL GROUPS

Moonraker, Dana Point, CA: (714) 855-2323, (714) 496-5891

Argonaut, Avalon, Catalina Island, CA; (213) 510-2208

Excalibur, Channel Islands Harbor, CA; (805) 529-4080

The Last Bite, Newport Beach/Long Beach, CA; (714) 832-8658

Hustler, San Diego, CA; (619) 222-0391, (619) 223-9729

Deep Thought, Santa Barbara, CA; (805) 967-4456

Pac-Man, San Diego, CA; (619) 575-3644

Sandy Bay, Channel Islands Harbor, CA; (213) 828-2418

Oceanus, Newport Beach, CA; (714) 646-2574

Vikingship, Marina Del Rey, CA; (213) 820-5657

Diavatis, Dana Point, CA; (714) 661-0320

Eagle, San Pedro, CA; (213) 832-9022

SCHEDULED DIVE TRIPS FOR GROUPS OF 20 OR MORE ON LARGE, FULLY-EQUIPPED BOATS

Truth, Santa Barbara Harbor, CA; (805) 962-1127

Conception, Santa Barbara Harbor, CA; (805) 962-1127

Vision, Santa Barbara Harbor, CA; (805) 962-1127

Peace, Ventura Harbor, CA; (805) 642-1393

Scuba Luv'er, Ventura Harbor, CA; (805) 496-1014

Spectre, Channel Islands Harbor, CA; (213) 833-1577, (818) 982-1334

Captain Midnight, Channel Islands Harbor, CA; (805) 642-7426

Barbara Marie, Channel Islands Harbor, CA; (805) 484-1594

Sea Ventures, Port Hueneme, CA; (805) 985-1100

Golden Doubloon, San Pedro, CA; (213) 831-5148

Wild Wave, San Pedro, CA; (213) 534-0034

Atlantis, San Pedro, CA; (213) 531-5582

Charisma, San Pedro, CA; (213) 326-7460

Cee Ray, San Pedro, CA; (213) 519-0880

Maverick, San Pedro, CA; (213) 547-3824

Scuba Queen, San Pedro, CA; (213) 691-0423

See Vue, San Pedro, CA; (714) 974-4272

Westerly, San Pedro, CA; (213) 833-6048

King Neptune, Avalon, Catalina Island, CA; (213) 510-0600

Mr. C, Long Beach, CA; (213) 831-9449

Electra, Oceanside, CA; (619) 722-2133

Bottom Scratcher, San Diego, CA; (619) 224-4997
Sand Dollar, San Diego, CA; (619) 224-4997
Horizon, San Diego, CA; (619) 277-7823

Catalina Island Services

FERRY SERVICES

Catalina Express, leaves from San Pedro, Berth 95, P.O. Box 1391, San Pedro, CA 90733; (213) 519-1212
Catalina Cruises, leaves from San Pedro and Long Beach, P.O. Box 1948, San Pedro, CA 90733
Catalina Passenger Service, leaves from Newport Beach; (714) 673-5245
California Cruisin', leaves from San Diego; (619) 235-8600

AIR SERVICES

Allied Air Charter, leaves from Long Beach Airport; (213) 510-1163
California Seaboard Airlines, leaves from Orange County; (714) 756-1020
Catalina-Vegas Airline, leaves from San Diego; (619) 272-7311
Helitrans (helicopter service), leaves from San Pedro; (800) 262-1472
Island Express (helicopter service), leaves from San Pedro and Long Beach; (213) 491-5550
Resort Commuter Airlines, leaves from Los Angeles and Orange County; (800) 523-3000

GENERAL INFORMATION

Catalina Island Chamber of Commerce and Visitor's Bureau, P.O. Box 217, Avalon, CA 90704; (213) 510-1520
California Department of Fish and Game (for current fish and game regulations), 1416 Ninth St., Sacramento, CA 95814; (213) 590-5132
Channel Islands National Park, 1901 Spinnaker Dr., Ventura, CA 93001; (805) 644-8157
Surface Tours of Channel Islands National Park, Island Packers Landing, 1867 Spinnaker Dr., Ventura, CA 93001; (805) 642-1393

Landing Permits

Santa Cruz Island—for western two-thirds of island, Santa Cruz Island Co., 515 S. Flower St., Los Angeles, CA 90071; for east end of island, c/o Mr. Pier Gherini, 1114 State St. #230, Santa Barbara, CA 93101
Santa Rosa Island—Vail & Vickers, 123 W. Padre St., Santa Barbara, CA 93105
San Miguel Island—Channel Islands National Park, 1901 Spinnaker Dr., Ventura, CA 93001; (805) 644-8157

Further Reading

Gotshall, D., and Laurent, L. *Pacific Coast Subtidal Marine Invertebrates.* Los Osos, California: Sea Challengers, 1979
Gotshall, D. *Pacific Coast Inshore Fishes.* Los Osos, California: Sea Challengers; Ventura, California: Western Marine Enterprises
California Diving News, monthly publication dedicated to California sport diving, P.O. Box 11231, Torrance, CA 90510

Index